T0167685

FIND YOUR FLOW

FOR MUM, DAD AND CHERI.

FIND

ESSENTIAL

YOUR

CHAKRAS

FLOW

SUSHMA SAGAR

POP PRESS

Contents

Introducing the Power of Chakras

What if I told you that you have a whole other secret world to explore that sits within you? What if you were given the keys to this world and those keys could help you flourish, prosper and enjoy your life even more? Life is a miracle, but it can also be frustrating, exhausting, lonely and upsetting at times. It's no wonder we all want to know how to live better. The extraordinary thing is there is more to you than what you can *actually see*. As human beings, we are far more than our cells and bones – we are energy beings living in a human body, and the keys to this being and body of ours lie in our chakras.

Our chakras are energy centres that can unlock our health and happiness. Even though your body already has the ability to tune itself intuitively using its chakras, a bit of understanding and guidance can amplify this inherent knowledge and give you a framework and support system that you can rely on. It will open you up further and enhance your connection to the world and everything in it. Once you start working with energy and your chakras, the universe has an uncanny ability to adjust your trajectory and change your life for the better. The wisdom of your energy body will move you and you'll find yourself getting better, quite simply, at being you.

What this Book Offers You

This book is a starter guide to understanding and connecting with your energy centres or chakras – which are the most underrated but important aspect of your being. Our chakras determine our entire lives and what happens in them, from how you feel to how you act, how you relate to others, what you achieve, how much you care, how you perceive life and how connected you feel to the universe. Your chakras are the sheet music that creates the melody of you; they are the shades of colour that create the painting of you; the behind-the-scenes crew responsible for the festival of you! Your chakras are intrinsic to your mental, physical, emotional and spiritual health, and every day, your experiences are determined by the behaviour of your chakras. By getting to know these essential parts of your being, you can live your best life – you can become a masterpiece!

You may have already heard about chakras, because they are talked about in many different schools of thought – from yoga to meditation to Ayurveda and Chinese medicine. However, this book is not about suggesting or focusing on any one tradition of wisdom or learning. After two decades of study and personal practice – from training as a master teacher in various forms of healing, to graduating as a shamanic energy medicine woman in a Peruvian Inca tradition and studying meditation with a master on the banks of the Ganges in India – I have come to realise that all traditions are connected and that they all have an understanding and appreciation of our energetic bodies. They all deal with 'the subtle self', a self that goes beyond our skin and bones; a self that goes further than what we can see with our eyes. The subtle self is the key to our state of being: how happy we are, how our life feels and how easily things flow to us.

Tuning in to Your Life Force

You may be wondering if you need to have a 'gift' or be part of a long line of witches to work with your own energy. The answer is no! Anyone can do it. Connecting to our personal life force is completely natural because it comes with the package of our body. Not once in my teaching, or in the training and workshops I have attended over the years, did I ever meet a person who could not tune in to their flow. It's an inherent skill and works through intention and intuition. For example, when your mother laid her hands on you when you were sick as a child, did you not feel better? She instinctively knew which chakra was imbalanced and how to comfort you through her own energy.

This book is intended to explain the workings of this fascinating part of our being – this whole hidden aspect of ourselves. My intention is to share with you my understanding of the principles and methods that I have been taught by incredible teachers over the last twenty years. I will aim to distil this wisdom in a way that makes sense in everyday terms. For instance, how does all this apply to you when you're losing your mind in the bagging area or dealing with social-media comparisons? Or if your partner dumps you or when you're feeling a bit flat? I hope to not only explain what chakras are and why they matter, but more importantly, show you how to work with them to get the best out of your life now, in the twenty-first century.

What are Chakras?

Chakras are powerful energy centres situated within our body. These points were named 'chakras' in Sanskrit, the ancient language of India. The direct translation is 'wheel' but the name 'chakra' has stuck across the world. The chakras form our inner engine, the cogs in the bigger wheel that makes up our energy system. We have seven major chakras in the body and another two directly above the body. There are, in fact, even more chakras, but for the purposes of this book we'll be concentrating on these ones.

The chakras form the skeleton structure of our energetic body, which sits inside our physical body. Though our physical and energy bodies are separate structures, they are symbiotic and work in harmony. Our physical state affects our energetic state and vice versa. Our energy body, however, can separate from our physical body if we want it to. If you have ever had an 'out of body' experience, you have experienced a separation of your energy body from your physical being.

When we are born, our energetic chakra structure exists in its infancy, but as we develop, each chakra grows and matures in turn, over a period of seven years, corresponding to what is happening in our lives at that time.

The Chakra System within Us

The first three chakras relate to the development of our physical body and our reaction to the external world. Our ego, which is where our personality and sense of self exist, is in charge of these areas. What our personal situation looks like, what we need, how we behave and how we feel we fit in with the world are all dependent on the development and behaviour of these chakras.

The next three belong to the soul, which is where we form our vision of our internal selves. This is where we become inspired and become an inspiration for others. The soul is the part of us that lives in our body and animates us – it is what makes us 'us'. This is where we find the seeds of our uniqueness and where we allow them to bloom so that we can share this with others. In these chakras, we feel an openness that goes beyond any ego-related issues.

Then the following three chakras connect us to spirit, which is the energy of the world that lives outside us. Spirit describes the greater, kind and intelligent force in the universe. Connecting to spirit is something that happens when we go beyond ourselves, our ego and our soul, and this is where we reach the divine. You don't need to be religious to do this, although many people have found their access point to this connection through a faith.

The first chakra sits at the base of our spine and matures by the time we are seven years old. At this age, our primary concern is survival, ensuring that we have enough food, warmth and protection. Safety is the biggest motivation and any sort of upset or neglect will affect the growth of this chakra. The manifestation of our material world and our base instincts are created at this age. What happens in the early part of our lives is crucial as it sets us up for the rest of our development.

The second chakra sits just below our navel and develops during the ages of seven to fourteen. It refers to our creative force and pleasure. Our most sensitive years, when we reach puberty and grow into young adults, are often fraught with difficulties, school problems and parental challenges. These changes and the examples we are set by those around us play an important role here. We are learning to enjoy life, to create and experiment with who we are becoming. We are learning what our nature is.

The third chakra sits below our ribcage and develops during the ages of fourteen to twenty-one. This is the period of the manifestation of action and our will. It's where we learn to stand up for ourselves, we start to wield our power and assert the nature that we have developed. It's a time when we decide what we care about, what is important to us and then stand up for it. Issues at school, college or home in which we might have been disempowered in any way may affect the growth of this chakra.

The fourth chakra forms a halfway bridging point in the body, where we move into the higher soul aspects and our internal worlds. It sits in the centre of our chest in our heart area and is fully formed between the ages of twenty-one to twenty-eight. It deals with love and compassion. This is the period of life when we learn that it's not all about us! Being able to reach beyond ourselves to support others can bring a sense of real joy, but if our hearts are broken, that can lead to this chakra becoming closed – something I am sure that many of us have experienced.

The fifth chakra sits in the throat and matures during the ages of twenty-eight to thirty-five. It deals with authenticity and its maturation occurs at a time when we become fully fledged adults with our own world view – one that goes beyond those we have inherited or absorbed from our culture or society. During this period of our life, we learn to take others' views into consideration, to understand our own and then communicate that to the world. Authenticity and finding your own voice are what happens here. Sadly, many people fear the consequences of speaking freely, which affects how this chakra behaves – constant throat issues are an indication of this.

The sixth chakra sits in our forehead and matures during the ages of thirty-five to forty-two. It deals with insights that come from within. The 'sixth sense' is the language of the sixth chakra. This sense is super helpful as it is the inner compass that tells us what we need to know and helps us intuitively find our direction in life. This chakra is where hunches live, and it's where you can see through nonsense at five paces. If it's blocked, you won't trust your intuition.

The seventh chakra, on the crown of our head, matures between the ages of forty-two to forty-nine and is where we connect to the universe and receive downloads of wonder. At the crown, we can see the beauty in everything and everyone; we have a higher vantage point from which to view the world. We can observe the bigger picture from a bird's eye view – how everything connects. We can perceive the expanded map of our lives.

The eighth and ninth chakra are situated outside the body and sit directly above our heads. This is where things get really cosmic! These chakras are our connection to the spirit of all that is and all that was and all that will be. The imprint of our lives and our potential reside in these upper chakras, and this is where we can access all the gems we need to fulfil our potential with the support of the entire universe. Insight and knowing – it's like being best friends with the head librarian and getting access to the private documents of your existence.

At each stage of our life, our chakras mature until finally we have all that we need to cope with every part of life.

The Energy In and Around Us

In order to talk about chakras, we must first talk about energy. The entire universe is made of energy. Albert Einstein outlined this when he wrote $E=MC^2$. He was able to prove that everything in the universe is made of energy, but that this energy exists in different forms. Energy can be transferred or transformed, but it can never die completely – it's a great model for sustainability. All living things, including us, are made of energy: we are energy beings. Every cell in our body is made of energy vibrating at a particular frequency. The faster the vibration, the better the flow of energy around our bodies; and the heavier the vibration, the slower the flow of energy around our bodies. Energy can even become blocked, which will affect our well-being.

The energy that flows around our body is like the unseen fuel that makes us ... well ... alive! Our energy affects our moods and impacts our experience of life. One day we might feel full of beans, the next we feel flat; the highs and lows of everyday life are governed by our energy flow. Energy is an invisible force that makes its presence known by affecting how we feel. Just because you can't see something doesn't mean it's not there – you use Wi-Fi, don't you?

How we come across to people is also dependent on our energy – and you will definitely have experienced this before. I'm talking about the vibes someone gives off before you have even been introduced to each other. If you decide you dislike someone from a distance, it might be because you have an aversion to their facial hair, but it's more likely because you have tuned in to their energy and made an invisible, subconscious judgement call.

Your energy field broadcasts to the world how you actually are. There is no way of hiding how you feel and pretending to be 'fine' when you are not. It's literally like walking around with a sandwich board displaying your state at all times. Revealing? Yes. Embarrassing? Sometimes. Seductive? Well, if you are looking for a partner, this can be very handy because it's our energy that often attracts someone before any words have been spoken.

Our energy fields are also stretchy and they can extend out several feet around us when we are feeling happy. On a good day, our vibrations can reach out so far that we attract correspondingly pleasing things to us. It's great like that. These are the days when people smile at you for no reason, all the traffic lights seem to be on green and you are given a free coffee at Pret. But, oh, when you are having a bad day, it can work the opposite way. Your energy field shrinks and feels heavy. You stub your toe, lose your keys, you are late for work and attract all the moaners in the office.

If someone is standing very close to us, we often say they are 'invading our personal space'. It can make you feel really uncomfortable, almost as though they are actually touching you. This is because in energetic terms they are! Their energy field is touching yours and, unless you really know and like them, it can feel invasive.

So, our experience of life is directly influenced by our energetic state. Life becomes a mirror for everything that is going on inside us. With that in mind, if you want something in your life to change on the outside (such as your home, friends, life, love interest, job – anything), you need to work on changing the energy on the inside, so you can become the frequency of what you want. Like attracts like!

The Universal Life Force

Working with energy is an ancient and universal technique. Traditions from all over the world agree that we are spiritual beings wrapped up in a physical body. I witnessed this first-hand when I studied in Mexico and saw how shamans used energy medicine as something that was completely normal. I also spent time in India studying the chakras, and it was here that I learned that energy medicine, arguably the original medicine for health and wellness, was well documented in Sanskrit texts dating back to 5000BC. The famous sage Patanjali talked of the hidden energy system in the body and the chakras were described in detail in the ancient Indian texts called the Vedas.

Chakras and our energy system form a major part of the yogic teachings; this may well be where you have heard about them. Yoga has become very well known in the West over the last few decades, but its true roots are not always understood here. Yoga is part of the Ayurvedic system of health, which holds that we are holistic beings and that to be healthy we must balance our mind, body and soul. Yoga is actually an ancient philosophical, physical and spiritual practice that was created to help people connect with the divine. It works to bring balance and flow to our chakra system, so it can give us a great energy body as well as a great physical body!

Throughout the ages, there have been extraordinary individuals who have been able to see the flow of energy in the body, to the extent that they could draw diagrams of where these energy channels lay. The ancient Indian medical men Charaka (born c.300BC) and Sushruta (born c.800BC) didn't need science to validate what they could perceive; it is believed that Sushruta, for example, was able to work with the internal organs, to operate and do complex surgery without the need for X-rays, simply by knowing where the body's energy flow lay. Chinese medicine concurs with this approach and today acupuncturists, for example, work with a complete system of pathways, or meridians, through which energy travels around the body.

It doesn't matter where we go in the world, the general consensus is the same; whether it's called chi, qi, prana, or the Holy Wind – it's all part of the same thing: energy. Energy is the life force of our being and the currency of our chakras. Whatever the dressing or the wrapping, the bare bones (pardon the pun) of the matter are that we are more than flesh and bone. We have an energy force that flows through us and which is intrinsic to how we function and how we feel. Working with chakras is an ancient wellness technique and our energy is the secret source (or sauce) of life!

Chakras as Our Energy Wheels

So, we have established that we are energy beings living in a world that is also made of energy. Our cells are made of energy; they vibrate at a frequency and they respond to energy when it is applied to them.

Think of the chakras as wheels. When they are healthy, they spin clockwise and draw energy into our bodies to be used as needed, just like water being sucked into a plughole. When they are imbalanced, they will spin slowly or not at all. They may even spin backwards when they are really clogged.

We connect directly to energy through our chakras in three different ways:

moving energy around the body;
letting energy in;
sending energy out.

MOVING ENERGY AROUND THE BODY

The chakras are connected by a network of thousands of energy pathways that exist in the body. The pathways are known as nadis. They allow energy to travel around the body and they meet in the first seven chakras. There is one main channel up the spine and two smaller channels that twist around it, carrying different types of energy around the body. The nadis connect and integrate with the main channels and the chakras to create an energetic infrastructure.

LETTING ENERGY IN

The chakras are also where we let energy in. They are the focal points that allow us to connect to the rest of the world. They are gateways or portals that behave like vortexes linking our physical bodies to our energy bodies and our energy bodies to the outside world. Seven spinning sockets that plug each of us into the universe to draw in or dispense energetic fuel.

SENDING ENERGY OUT

The chakras also allow us to send energy outwards. We can send love and good vibes, or hate and bad vibes, and we can do both of these things, consciously or unconsciously, simply through our thoughts. Which of these we do depends on our intentions. Our intentions are the motivations behind our actions. The same energy that can wish someone well can also wish ill. You are so powerful that your thoughts can determine whether that energy will hurt or heal. Your motives can quite literally move mountains behind or in front of people.

Chakras and Our Physical and Emotional Bodies

This energetic system is designed to work in harmony with the physical body, with each chakra overseeing an area of the body that relates to a gland. I find it so interesting that the physical function in the body mirrors the chakra function. For example, the pancreas in the stomach deals with the digestion of food, while the solar plexus chakra, which is also in the stomach, deals with the digestion of a situation. It makes a lot of sense.

The chakras also relate to aspects of our emotional health and this is where you may find most success working with them in normal life. On a day-to-day basis, we feel a roller coaster of emotions and we need to support ourselves to navigate these highs and lows. How we feel has a direct correlation to how healthy our chakra is. For example, if we have been hurt, our heart chakra may close and we will have a feeling of heaviness or numbness in our chest. If we are stressed, we may feel it in the bottom of our stomach – and that relates to our second chakra. We can feel our energetic health if we tune in to our physical health and we can positively affect our physical health by supporting our energetic health.

What do Chakras look like?

Ancient yogic drawings depict the chakras as funnels that begin in our backbones and open out perpendicularly above the body – except for the first chakra, which points downwards to the floor. You may have seen chakras drawn as wheels, or as beautiful, flower-like mandalas to represent their spiritual meanings.

In our bodies, the chakras usually measure around 10cm (4in) in diameter, but they can grow or diminish depending on their health. The first chakra is situated at the bottom of our tailbone and they work their way upwards, governing sections of our body, until they reach the top of our head – the crown. The upper two chakras sit above our heads in our energy fields, which extend beyond the body. The eighth chakra is often depicted as a big halo or orb above the head and the ninth is usually simply shown as an area in our energy field, directly above the eighth chakra.

The chakras spin at different speeds, with the lower chakras spinning slower than the higher ones. They are usually depicted in colour because the frequency of each one corresponds to a particular colour. Like a pantone chart, chakra energy exists in a range of beautiful colours: red, orange, yellow, green, sky blue, indigo, lilac, gold and white. These colours actually exist inside us – we are quite literally walking, talking rainbows of light energy!

What do Chakras feel like?

How your chakras feel will depend on their health.
A happy, spinning chakra will feel light and fluid in your
body. A blocked or imbalanced chakra will feel heavy
and stuck and, if left long enough, will eventually lead
to a physical symptom. For example, if you have been
ruminating and worrying incessantly about something
for hours, you will block your sixth chakra and that will
become a headache! You can actually feel your chakra if
you hold your hand about 10cm (4in) above your body –
the air will feel a little different, buzzier or fuzzier. Later
in the book, I will share exercises that you can practise.

The chakras respond beautifully to the vibrations of other
substances. In fact, there are a myriad of ways to connect
with your chakras – from the colour you wear, to the
vibration of an essential oil or crystal, the effect on the
body of a particular yoga pose or through the emotions
of a meditative visualisation. From breathwork to healing,
we are spoilt for choice when it comes to working with
the energies of our chakras.

How can Working with My Chakras Help Me?

Most of us bumble through life, oblivious to the things that might be affecting us, but the minute we notice these silent influences, it's as if a world of opportunity is opening up – an opportunity to heal any old gripes, grudges, upsets and wounds that may be affecting our chakras and our flow, and to help us feel better about everything. We may notice that we have stress or tension in a part of our body and we can work with our chakras to address it. Working with a chakra is like exercising a muscle: the more you do it, the stronger it gets.

Let's also not forget that each of us has a huge impact on those around us. The echoes of our state of mind and body reverberate around us and affect those we come into contact with. The people we love will be directly affected by how we are, so it stands to reason that if we want to be a better partner, mother, father, sister, brother or friend, we should work on managing our own energy and our own selves. Simply by living in a higher, healed vibration, and by finding our own flow, we can help and inspire others around us through our mere existence.

When life is easy and things happen without much effort, we are in a state of grace, in the flow of the universe and everything seems to be going our way. The state we are in depends on our attitudes, how energy is moving through us and therefore how our chakras are functioning. The more we can keep our chakras healthy, balanced and spinning correctly, the more we will find things flowing for us.

Health goes way beyond our physical self; it extends into how we live. By adopting this approach to health, we can develop awareness and sensitivity of this unseen aspect of our being. To improve our quality of life, we don't necessarily need more stuff or more status; just a simple yet enhanced awareness of our subtle selves – and with this insight, the keys to the universe lie within our reach. Hands up, who fancies that?

You are Your Home

When you think about your home, you might think of the four walls and roof under which you reside, but what about the skin in which you live? You were given a physical body as your home for this lifetime, so let's consider your energy body, where your chakras sit, as being yet another home that you live in.

Picture this: your energy body is a shimmering hologram of a beautiful, multistorey, rainbow house that belongs to you. Imagine you have the keys to an entire building that you have never completely explored. Let's say that each chakra relates to a different level of that building, occupying a room on it. The openings to the chakras are like windows that allow energy to come in from the universe and go out from us. They need to be fully functional, shiny and clean, so you can open and close them, as well as see in and out of them with ease.

You are powered by energy that travels around your chakras via pathways. In our house analogy, let's imagine that each room on each of the floors is interconnected with a set of main power cables (the nadi). There is a central channel called the Sushumna, which carries the main energy to fuel the whole house. There are also two smaller channels, called Ida and Pingala. Ida carries the flow of feminine and creative energy on the left side of the body, whereas Pingala is the masculine flow, the energy of logic and action on the right. These cables switch sides around the sixth floor, the level where our head would be in a human body, which is why the left side of our brain controls our logical, rational thinking and our right hemisphere controls our creative thinking.

We are going to explore the chakras as if we were exploring our house, floor by floor, but it's important to note that we are greater than the sum of our separate parts. Even though each chakra is individual, they are all completely interlinked – they come as a whole. We need to take responsibility for the upkeep of the entire energetic home and, in doing so, we will enhance our experience of life.

So, we need to keep every floor of the house in good order and each level needs to be tidy and clean. If one floor isn't well cared for, the whole house will suffer. By understanding what makes up each part of our home – the nuances, the unseen aspects of our being – we can fast-track our way through the queues of life and it will become a whole lot more enjoyable as a result.

The Nine
Chakras

The First Chakra – the Root Chakra

The first chakra is called the root chakra or 'Muladhara' in Sanskrit, which means 'foundation'. It sits at the bottom of your tailbone and literally forms the base of your energy home. Like the sub-structure of a house, this chakra goes far into the earth to provide stability and strength for the whole building. If its foundations are deep and strong, it will withstand earthquakes and floods, so even in a life storm, your house won't fall down. The root chakra is arguably one of the most important chakras in that it keeps you solid and upright.

This chakra is concerned with your basic existence and survival, such as having enough food, shelter, warmth – the absolute basics that we need to exist. It is the place where you might keep stocks of rice and toilet roll, so to speak.

This chakra fully matures up until the age of seven, which is why we can see babies and small children operating at this level. They are instinctively aware of their survival; they know what they need and they will cry the house down if they don't get it. If you had any trauma when you were young, this could appear like a small crack in the concrete foundations of this chakra and could affect your stability later.

THE COLOUR AND ELEMENT

This chakra's colour is a deep, rich red, which anchors you into the earth. It is also linked to the element of earth, which makes perfect sense given its location and name. It stands to reason that grounding is a big part of working with this chakra. When we are grounded, we feel connected to the earth and we aren't flighty. It stops us feeling wobbly and insecure about life. This isn't about ideas; this is about reality. IRL.

THE PHYSICAL AND ENERGETIC CONNECTION

From a physical perspective, this chakra corresponds to the adrenal gland, which is responsible for your ability to fight or flee or freeze. In modern life, this could manifest in the somewhat unthreatening scenario of running to catch a bus or the scarier situation of having a fight with someone. Whether the stress is big or small, your body will support you by releasing the hormone adrenaline, so that you can use all your resources and focus them on removing the perceived threat.

From an energetic perspective, this is about the energy you need to handle fear. However, fear is meant to be like an alarm system in the home: once it sounds, you find the cause and then reset it. If you don't, your adrenaline alarm will be left to run continuously, which will wear it out and make the whole house stressful to be in, literally as if an alarm were sounding 24/7.

The root chakra is also concerned with the disposal of waste, because the waste disposal pipes that come from you are situated there too!

TELL-TALE SIGNS YOUR ROOT CHAKRA IS WORKING WELL (OR NOT)

When this chakra is strong and working well, you will feel grounded, stable and supported – like there's always going to be enough food in the supermarket for you to buy, you'll always be able to pay your rent and the heating will always be toasty. You feel confident that whatever happens, you will be able to handle it.

If this chakra is weak, it will show itself in behaviours such as never feeling fully secure or suffering from a scarcity issue. This is the fear where the thought of not having enough fills you with an irrational, bone-deep dread. It's crucial that children are given love and affection in their very early years, because this will create a secure adult who doesn't crave attention to try to fill a void that came from the cracks in their first chakra when it was developing.

The Second Chakra – the Sacral Chakra

The next chakra is known as the sacral chakra or 'Swadisthana' in Sanskrit, which translates as 'sweet dwelling place'. It sits just below your navel, between your hips, and takes in the reproductive area. It is concerned with emotions, sexuality and how you feel. Let's consider this to be your front garden – a beautiful lawn filled with flowers and flowing fountains, a sweet place to stay and be inspired. This chakra becomes fully formed by the age of fourteen and covers the time of puberty. It's a very interesting phase in life because we change dramatically from children into young adults. Through adolescence, we grow out of our awkwardness and our buds start to flower – our gardens blossom, so to speak. Pleasure and sensation are the essential features of the second chakra.

THE COLOUR AND ELEMENT

This chakra energy has the colour of orange, so picture orange flowers in your garden, bright and fragrant. The water flowing through this garden represents the element of water, which is assigned to this chakra. This is the place where we move, where the real flow happens. It's the place where we can build our desire to create. Our passions and our ability to grow ideas lie here.

THE PHYSICAL AND ENERGETIC CONNECTION

Interestingly, this chakra corresponds to the ovaries and testicular glands, so it's all about creation in both a physical and an energetic sense. Imagine how when you plant seeds in the ground, they will grow into flowers. In this second chakra, those seeds are ideas and emotions. This is about your mojo, both sexually and creatively, because ultimately the energy source for both is the same. We are often taught to feel ashamed about our pleasures, but abstaining completely from them because of a sense of guilt can lead to a weak chakra and this is incredibly damaging to the flow of energy: it will create an unhealthy block that will lead to destructive tendencies and a drought of creativity or passion.

TELL-TALE SIGNS YOUR SACRAL CHAKRA IS WORKING WELL (OR NOT)

This area also governs your boundaries so you know when to say 'yes' or 'no'. Imagine a small fence all around the garden that separates it from the public footpath. When you have a healthy and balanced second chakra, you have a great sense of self-respect. From refusing that extra drink to saying no to unwanted advances, this is actually about knowing what's right for you and what isn't. The boundary fence that separates you from the public footpath is literally the thing that stops people from stomping all over your garden!

A person with a weak second chakra may find it hard to say no, but this is not healthy and often leads to burnout rather than a promotion, for example. Women sadly often suffer from a weak second chakra because we are often socially conditioned to help, to say yes and to be as amenable as possible. The irony is that you tend to get more respect by having healthy boundaries and setting a polite precedent about how you want to be treated.

The Third Chakra – the Solar Plexus Chakra

The next chakra sits between your navel and chest. It is called the solar plexus chakra or 'Manipuri', which translates as 'lustrous gem'. This chakra is a shiny, powerful place where we can make things happen. It's concerned with action and doing, being assertive and self-sufficient. It's where we fuel a strong will to do something – and then we do it!

Using our house metaphor, let's think of it like a kitchen, where we take the ingredients or ideas that are grown in our garden and then, using fire, we cook up something delicious. This chakra matures between the ages of fourteen to twenty-one, which is usually when young adults decide what they want to do in the world. In my case, I became a vegetarian and joined Greenpeace because I felt hugely motivated to take action and make a difference.

THE COLOUR AND ELEMENT

The colour of this chakra is yellow and it relates to the element of fire! When it is powerful, strong and healthy, you will make your mark in the world. You will feel excited and enthused, but only if you have the balanced energy to take the right actions that will enable you to see your plans to fruition.

THE PHYSICAL AND ENERGETIC CONNECTION

It's interesting that the glands connected with this chakra are the pancreas and adrenals, which are concerned with digestion, metabolism and the energy to move quickly. Your digestion separates nutrients and expels waste as your body decides what is worth holding on to; and then you let go of the rest, which travels down the gut.

In terms of our lives and our energy, the solar plexus helps us to deal with situations. In this chakra, you are able to understand what is worth keeping and what is not. We often hold a lot of stress in our stomachs when we struggle against whatever is happening. Your ability to digest life, and therefore your motivation for life, sits in your solar plexus. Once you have accepted and made peace with whatever has happened, you can transform and act accordingly.

When you cook, you first need to assess what you have and then prepare your ingredients. You need to peel and remove the unnecessary parts before you can make the right dish. This peaceful acceptance leaves us free to act in complete integrity with ourselves and what is best for us, or, in other words, 'working out what is shit and then getting shit done', as my teacher used to say!

TELL-TALE SIGNS YOUR SOLAR PLEXUS CHAKRA IS WORKING WELL (OR NOT)

With an unbalanced solar plexus, either nothing much happens or too much happens. You might be overwhelmed with energy, but not grounded enough to be able to direct that energy constructively, which eventually leads to total apathy. For example, when you *really* like someone and you want to meet them, but your feelings have sent you into a spin and you can't decide what to wear, what to do or what to say – so you cancel. Alternatively, you may be so action-orientated that you turn power-hungry and impatient, lacking empathy and wanting everything yesterday. Your friends will likely give you a wide berth!

Whether you feel powerful or powerless will depend very much on the health of the solar plexus chakra. Keep that kitchen fire burning bright, but not out of hand.

These first three chakras are considered to be the lower chakras and vibrate at slower frequencies than those above them. As we ascend, we move with faster energies because we are dealing with lighter emotions, and we rise into higher planes of consciousness. We are now moving away from the aspects of our house that deal with the 'self' and into the upper floors of the house that deal with the 'soul'.

The Fourth Chakra – the Heart Chakra

Moving up, the next chakra is called the heart chakra and is known as 'Anahata', which means 'unbound'. It sits in the centre of your chest at the midpoint between the lower and higher chakras, and it deals with matters of love, compassion and connection. How we relate to each other and how much we care are both dealt with in this area. This is where we become untied from the shackles of need or desire and we are quite literally free to love and be loved. This chakra fully forms in our twenties, at a time when we may start to seek a partner or family. Whether you buy in to traditional role models or not, it's a time to experience genuine love. I imagine this chakra as a living room, where we gather together to engage with our loved ones.

The energy of love has three different vibrations. Many confuse having the hots for someone as love, but that is more about lust and it requires an exchange of some sort. It is primal and feeds off 'need and desire', so it lives instead in the lower chakras. The love we experience in the heart rises above this: it is a love for the sake of love. This love can be a non-sexual love – the kind we have for a family member or a small child, or for a situation, place or a thing. When we love without conditions, this is a pure, high-frequency emotion. It's a love that needs nothing else in order to exist.

THE COLOUR AND ELEMENT

This chakra energy is either green or pink, and I imagine this living room as a calm and peaceful space. It is a place to connect and engage, for affinity with others and where we bring things together in pure unity. This chakra is linked to the element of air and how much air flows into our chest. When we inhale deeply we can feel our hearts expand and soften as the air from our breath massages our heart chakra area and boosts it.

THE PHYSICAL AND ENERGETIC CONNECTION

Interestingly, this chakra also corresponds to the lungs, the heart and the thymus gland, which sit in the upper area of the chest. The heart has the strongest electromagnetic field in the body, six times stronger than any other organ, and it has a very powerful effect. When your heart expands from loving feelings, it sends vibrations of warmth and comfort around you – a gorgeous energy to wallow in. With those heartfelt emotions, you can relax and literally breathe more easily.

Touch is also an important aspect of this chakra. Hugs, physical connection and intimacy all boost the heart chakra. When we cuddle our pets or our children, it's doing as much for our heart chakra as it is in soothing theirs.

TELL-TALE SIGNS YOUR HEART CHAKRA IS WORKING WELL (OR NOT)

If you find yourself over-attached and co-dependent, this could be because you are still operating from a place of scarcity, where your foundations are not strong and they are affecting how you relate to others. A healthy heart does not need anything in order to love. It loves just because it can find this feeling inside itself. It loves all around it, because it knows that by doing so, it is loving itself. When you are operating from the heart, you can stop feeling upset about someone who may have hurt you and reach a place where you actually feel compassion for them. I know this to be true, I managed it with my ex!

A healthy fourth chakra makes for genuine exchange. The kind of relations that really move you, whether it's a heart-to-heart at 2am with your new 'best friend' at a party or something longer lasting with your beloved. This is the place where you will create profound friendships or relationships.

The Fifth Chakra – the Throat Chakra

The throat chakra is situated in the centre of the neck and is called 'Visshudha', which translates as 'purification' or 'purest of the pure'. It is concerned with communication and it is here where we express the purest essence of ourselves. Think of it as a creative studio. In order to make our mark on the world, we are able to give a voice to what is felt in the heart. This chakra fully forms by the age of thirty-five, and it's a time when we learn to communicate our real feelings to the outer world. And truth is really what this chakra is concerned with: being not only able to access our truth, but once we know what this is, being ready, willing and able to express it. Expressing our real selves involves uncovering our creativity and our originality – those aspects of ourselves that make us 'us' and which in turn allow for the authentic expression of who we are. It is sometimes said that inspiration comes from the universe; if that is true, this chakra allows you to be a voice or mouthpiece for the universal mind.

THE COLOUR AND ELEMENT

The colour of this chakra is pale blue, so picture lots of windows and skylights in your creative studio. This is where you can write, say or sing what's on your mind. It is where you have the space and freedom to express yourself however you want, be that through writing or art, through movement, speech or sound. Sound is the element of the fifth chakra and has more to do with energy than you might think. Many religions believe that before the world began, there was sound. The Big Bang theory proposes that following a colossal explosion a huge vibration created the world and everything in it. Sound is a form of creation so, with that in mind, all we need to do is think and communicate an idea for it to exist.

THE PHYSICAL AND ENERGETIC CONNECTION

Communication is happening all the time inside the busy hubs of your body, with incredible amounts of information being sent and received in multitudes of ways; these include micro messages from your hormones to your cells, data from your cells to your body, and impulses from your brain to your muscles. Then outside your body, there is a whole other show going on! You are sending messages to and receiving them from other people, using language and its timings, volume and tone, as well as through visual signals from your body movements and even more subtle signs from your energy and even the scent you may give off. So many vehicles, both seen and unseen, of which we are conscious or unconscious, all pooling together to communicate the truth of what you are, who you are and what is happening in you.

The fifth chakra is associated with the thyroid gland and this gland is about growth and metabolism in your body. When it is healthy you can metabolise your thoughts and ideas into expression; you grow as a human being. Disease comes when our energy system is disharmonious; Richard Gerber M.D., an expert in vibrational medicine, believes that disease is initiated in the energy body before physical symptoms occur. Gong baths, sound baths and tuning fork therapy all work by using the vibrations of sound to stimulate cells to arrange themselves harmoniously.

TELL-TALE SIGNS YOUR THROAT CHAKRA IS WORKING WELL (OR NOT)

When this chakra is working well, you use your voice to share what you think and you are not concerned about being right or wrong – your ability to communicate creatively flows with ease. You realise that everyone is right and everyone is wrong; it really is a case of perspective and intention. Communicating at this level involves integrity in what you say and how you say it – and that means being truly authentic. No fake news allowed here!

When the fifth chakra is not balanced, you have trouble saying what you truly mean. You may have a debilitating fear of public speaking or suffer from throat or thyroid problems. Many people will resonate with this block – it's very common because we are often brought up not to rock any boats with strong opinions. The good news is that these things can be overcome when you work with the energy and clear a way for it to move upwards.

The Sixth Chakra – the Third Eye

This chakra is known as the third eye and it sits in the middle of the forehead, just between the eyebrows. Its name in Sanskrit is 'Anja', which means 'to perceive'. This refers to the ability to see with closed eyes through the third eye, and to internal sight; it is the sixth chakra that gives us our sixth sense. This chakra will have fully matured by your early forties and I was taught that it is the leader of the other chakras.

Let's consider this to be the room at the top of the house, which has windows through which we can see all around, both inside and out. This is the room where we close our eyes, but see even further, inside our minds. I like to think of this chakra as being like a bedroom, a place where we can sleep, dream and intuit, understanding our past, present and, most importantly, our future.

This is where seeing takes on a different quality and it refers to how we receive information about what is happening and therefore how we understand the world. Perception is a broader term for this faculty and inner sight might be another way of describing it. It's that sensation when you just 'know' things that you haven't been told about. You can read between the lines. It can occur when something doesn't seem quite right or when you have a feeling about a person you've just met and know that they will be important to you.

Have you ever made a major decision because something inside you said it was the right thing to do? You had a hunch and, without rhyme or reason, you went for it and it worked out really well? That means your third eye was on form, giving you a heads-up about what was right for you.

THE COLOUR AND ELEMENT

The colour of this chakra is indigo, a peaceful, deep blue which reaches into the depths of our minds. It's no coincidence that blue is used as a calming colour in public spaces – it is a shade that helps to bring peace to our hectic minds. The element associated with this chakra is light and light is the food of your third eye – meaning the light that comes in not through your eyes, but behind your eyes in the pineal gland.

THE PHYSICAL AND ENERGETIC CONNECTION

The pineal gland works by taking in light – and that is how this chakra functions. Just as eyes take in light and translate that light into visual information to give us a picture of the outside world, so the pineal gland creates a picture in the form of an inner knowing. It also governs our ability to sleep.

Intuition is the ability that comes from this inner sight. It's the skill of understanding a scenario without any obvious clues, of getting to the essence of a person, place or thing; for example, of knowing which passport queue is going to be the quickest or which job offer to take when they are both pretty good. In general, it's the inner compass that allows you to make the best decisions for yourself. Your third eye is like another antenna through which you can reach out into the universe and see other truths. What you think is absolutely key in keeping this chakra flowing nicely – your thoughts are literally the food of the third eye chakra and affect how its energy flows.

TELL-TALE SIGNS YOUR THIRD EYE CHAKRA IS WORKING WELL (OR NOT)

This is a very sensitive chakra, so if you start to get into a spin about issues concerning the lower chakras, it will become blocked, which can lead to insomnia and headaches. This is why it's really important to work on the lower chakras before moving upwards. The grime from the lower chakras will blow up and make the windows of this room extremely dirty, stopping you from seeing out. Using the practices given later in this book, keep all your windows gleamingly clean, so you can see with ease, both inside and out.

In order to keep this chakra working well, you need to be your own thought police and monitor what's running through your head to keep its energies positive and uplifting. Every time you go down a road of negative thinking and give an audience to guilt, doubt, fear, unhappiness or comparison, be aware that these thoughts will literally kill your third eye's ability to see through the clouds. You have an in-built compass, but it will not work if your mind is full of heavy and draining thoughts.

When this chakra is balanced, you will feel a sense of knowing, which will allow you to glide through life understanding instinctively what to do and when, without the need for validation or proof. You will know in yourself what is best for you and instinctively make the right decisions. You trust your inner guidance system and you believe in yourself. When you live life acting from a deep sense of trust, the world reconfigures to give you what is good for you.

The Seventh Chakra – the Crown Chakra

The crown chakra sits on the very top of your head. In Sanskrit, this chakra is known as 'Sahasrara', which means 'emptiness'. Think of it as being like a roof terrace, a place where we can bask in the rays coming down from above. Where the root chakra connects us directly with the earth, the crown chakra connects us to the sky and a universal source of energy. By the time we are forty-nine years old, it should have fully matured. This chakra is all about transcendence and illumination – our understanding of existence.

The crown chakra acts like an entry point for all the good stuff to come through to us from the cosmos. We can lie back and receive; we can bask in the sun and enrich our entire systems in the healthy glow of the universe. It's a portal to heaven, if you like.

When we operate from the seventh chakra and beyond, we are working with a higher, soulful perspective at all times. We are connected to everything and everyone, and the energy and the wisdom of this takes us to a place of total selflessness.

THE COLOUR AND ELEMENT

The colour of the crown chakra is pale violet, almost like a spectrum of all colours, and its element is energy – this is about infinity and space. It is to do with integrity, wisdom and selflessness. The seventh chakra has nothing to do with the physical body or ego – you are beyond that now, floating as part of something vast and unknowable, open to the universe.

THE PHYSICAL AND ENERGETIC CONNECTION

The crown chakra has no physical perspective; it is where you reach into the heavens and open yourself up to whatever wonderful vibrations are coming down into you. You connect to consciousness and you tune in to the divine. You realise that your existence is sacred and you are everything and everything is you.

Have you ever felt a deep inspiration or feeling of oneness that goes beyond anything you have felt before – where you feel illuminated? Unless you are an enlightened being like Buddha, it's unlikely that you are living full-time in this mode – for most mortals, these moments are fleeting. In the lower chakras we are preoccupied with the self, but up here we move beyond all that, into the realm of the spirit.

TELL-TALE SIGNS YOUR CROWN CHAKRA IS WORKING WELL (OR NOT)

You'll know when your seventh chakra is working well because you feel as if you are connected to the universe. You will feel open and ready to receive energy through the top of your head. You feel connected to a higher form of flow, so you receive insights easily and you'll notice ideas constantly coming through your crown. This is about a connection with the realm of spirituality. It is absolutely not about you any more. You can regard life from a higher perspective and you can let go and give yourself to the flow of life. (I sometimes feel like this after a yoga class when I'm relaxing in Savasana, the final pose when you simply surrender and lie on your back.)

When this chakra is not working well, you will be too consumed with yourself and the material world. This may eventually make you feel as if your life lacks lustre, as though something is missing: that something is inspiration, spirituality and magic.

It's important to understand that you need to have built and supported the lower chakras in order to get to this chakra: you must address the imbalances of the lower chakras in order to move past them. Then you will find a place where you genuinely no longer care about desire, regret or need; when you have you left all of those concerns behind and it feels like a relief to have no more attachment to any worldly worries. In this chakra, you learn to give in to the flow completely – you learn to trust, really trust, in the universe. You have found faith in a greater power and understand that this power has our best interests at heart. You learn that the universe is a friendly place and you truly believe that it will give us whatever will serve us best.

This is the place people find themselves when their entire world has collapsed and they turn to God, but why wait for such a crisis and use religion to get there? We can find that place inside ourselves, even when things are good.

The Eighth and Ninth Chakras – the Soul Star and the Mouth of God

The eighth and ninth chakras were revealed to me through my shamanic work. They are not the chakras that govern our physical life on the earth; they have nothing to do with the workings of the body, but they do hold information about them.

You may like to think of these chakras as enhanced vehicles that connect you to the cosmos and the realm of spirit. We tend not to work directly with these in our everyday life, but you may experience them at moments of spiritual bliss and those experiences in your deepest sleep or through meditation where your spirit has transcended – this is where you return to where we originally came from.

The eighth chakra is known as the Soul Star. It is a big tank of light and energy, a source of the sacred. In terms of our house analogy, you could think of it as the solar panels on your roof, which receive and hold an infinite supply of light energy from the universe and the cosmos. This is beyond everything on the earthly plane. In actual fact, it's like a big orb above your crown chakra: you can actually reach up and feel it. You may have seen religious paintings with figures who have halos above their heads – a depiction of them with their eighth chakra visible.

The ninth chakra is referred to as the Mouth of God and it is where we can access all that is. It's akin to a big server that holds the information about our incarnations. Many believe our spirits come from the stars and that we live many lifetimes – and that the details of these lives are held in the ninth chakra. The imprint of everything we are and ever have been is held there. The essence of our spirit, the iterations of our souls in various lifetimes can be accessed in this magical place.

THE COLOUR AND ELEMENT

The eighth chakra is the colour of gold and its element is soul. The ninth has no colour. It is white light and its element is spirit.

THE PHYSICAL AND ENERGETIC CONNECTION

There is no physical element because the eighth and ninth chakras are about pure energy and consciousness.

TELL-TALE SIGNS YOUR SOUL STAR AND MOUTH OF GOD CHAKRAS ARE WORKING WELL (OR NOT)

You will feel a sense of liberation from the heavy day-to-day gunk of earthly life and you will feel as if you are connected to the heart of the universe. You will feel like your purest self, beyond matter, beyond consciousness, just pure spirit. There is no such state as either working well or not working well at this point; everything just is.

Health and Harmony for Mind, Body and Soul

The natural way of keeping your chakras in check is through a holistically balanced lifestyle. This concept was originally cited in Ayurvedic manuscripts that discuss the harmony of mind, body and soul for our total health. We need our home to operate cohesively, with each floor working separately for whatever function it was designed for, but also as a place where every part of life is dealt with, so we can live harmoniously. It's essential that we consider the whole house – that is, our entire selves.

The easiest way to keep all our chakras in balance is through our minds and attitudes. What we think is certainly one of the most important factors. In her book *Molecules of Emotion,* neuroscientist Candace B. Pert explores the behaviour of cells and determines that emotions have the ability to change the molecular structure of our cells. That's right, I'll say it again: our thoughts actually control the behaviour of the cells in our body. Happy, positive thoughts boost energy in the body – they affect how a cell grows, supporting its best evolution. Conversely, if we are stressed and unhappy, this adversely affects the cells: scientific studies have proven that this emotional state can increase the propensity to inflammation, which is the cause of disease. Keeping our emotions in check is the secret to good health and good energy flow around the body, avoiding the energy drain that comes from being on a downer.

In his book *The Cosmic Energy & Chakras,* meditation master Dev OM writes that the natural way to maintain a healthy chakra system is to be fully conscious of all parts of ourselves. We need to be aware of what we think and therefore what we feel. We must also consider what we consume, what we achieve and how much we move our body; by considering all of these areas, we keep our entire house tidy and the energy flowing.

How We Feel

How we feel is a state of mind – and it is completely within our control. It's a choice and a habit, so we can decide how we want to be and then be that. It's so simple and it's entirely up to us. Happiness isn't based on what we have or don't have, which is why some of the richest people in the world don't seem to be content and satisfied with their lot. Feelings of happiness, joy, freedom, peace and love generate high vibrational energy in the body, which is the premium fuel and feeds all our chakras.

What We Eat

We have a physical body and this is also our home, so we need to ensure that the actual matter of which we are made is well sustained. We are what we eat: it quite literally becomes us! What we digest determines whether we feel healthy. The nutrients in the food we consume, and how processed or natural they are, determines the value of what is absorbed by our body – and this too plays a role in how well energy moves around our system. Food has different energies based on how much it has been processed and cooked.

Each person is individual and has different nutritional needs, so I am in no way suggesting that you stop eating any particular food or stop having takeaways ... sometimes! This is about simply having an awareness of the impact of food on your body. Eating consciously is a very different state of awareness to mindlessly shovelling in anything and it's this awareness of what you consume that will support the flow of energy in your body.

It is interesting to note, however, that different foods do have an effect on different chakras, often depending on how quickly these foodstuffs move through us. Meats and animal products tend to take longer to digest and therefore they slow us down, but they can also ground us if we are too flighty. If overeaten, refined sugars, even those found in carbohydrates such as pasta, can have a detrimental effect on our third chakra, the solar plexus chakra, and weaken the flow of energy in us. Vegetables on the whole take in light from the sun to grow, so when we consume them we ingest all that goodness from their cells. Fruits also move through our bodies quickly and leave us nourished with vitamins. Energy can pass more quickly to the upper chakras the quicker and more easily we digest these foods.

How Much We Move

If we don't use it, we lose it! We need to keep our physical body moving – and movement is a key part of helping energy to flow around our body. Energy in the form of emotions can get stuck in joints; have you ever felt like crying after a yoga class or some dynamic stretching? (I do all the time!) That's due to a release of trapped emotions and it's so good to get these out. The release of endorphins that comes from exercise makes us happy and, yes, feeling good is energetic fuel.

What We Achieve

When we feel as if we have completed something, we feel mentally at rest. Peace of mind and contentment are a huge part of keeping our energy flowing easily and naturally. Feeling satisfied with what we have done, whether helping a child with homework, reading another chapter of a book or simply cleaning the house – it doesn't matter what it is – but getting things done that we want to get done makes us feel great, which, in turn, keeps our energy flowing. Whatever is on your to-do list, try to tick something off each day.

These may feel like very general notions and you may be wishing I could give you a strict routine to adhere to that would immediately sort out your chakras completely and forever, but sadly this wouldn't work for a number of reasons. Firstly, no one likes being told exactly what to do all the time, so you would probably try the routine for a bit and then stop. Secondly, I don't know you or who you are, how you feel, look, think and behave. Things are constantly moving and changing, so what works for you one day may not feel right the next – one size doesn't fit all. Working with your chakras is really about getting to know yourself and what feels good for you. I am happy to give you some ideas and pointers here and you can use the chakra prescriptions later on in the book, but, ultimately, when you start to become aware of your own energy and how things affect it, you will be able to use your own judgement about what's working and what isn't. You will be your own housekeeper.

This is about developing a deeper awareness of everything you say, eat, do and think. All of those elements need to be working together to bring you to your best emotional, physical and spiritual health. Of course, it's a tall order to expect everyone to have this down perfectly – after all, we are human, we are flawed and we forget! But like any habit, it's only formed through repetition, so the more times you keep a check on yourself, the less times you will need to. This is like cleaning as you go along rather than waiting for a big mess to build up before you tackle it.

Creating an Environment for Flow

Even though we are talking about chakras and energy flow, let's not forget how much our actual physical environment can affect us. We have established that our overall chakra health can be positively affected by our mood and it's crucial to remember that our environment can be a large part of that. The energy of our space can have a huge effect on how we feel and how we flow. There is a whole world of information out there about decluttering and the like, but in a general sense we are trying to stay happy – and that's the bottom line. It's much easier to feel better when you make your bed in the morning, when your space is neat, tidy and clean. Dust and musty air hold heavy energies, so to clean the energetic space, you must also clean the physical space.

Take a look around you. What brings you up and what brings you down? Remove any items that make your heart sink. These could be photos of an ex-partner, something that was given to you that you don't actually like but feel guilty about not keeping, or something that needs mending which makes you feel bad whenever you look at it. Remove them from your eye line and make a point of either dealing with or dispensing with them sooner rather than later. Try to keep only uplifting things in your view, so that your emotions stay positive.

Here are a couple of simple practices to help you get your house in order, energetically speaking.

TAKE STOCK OF YOUR ENERGY SYSTEM

Let's start at the beginning. If you were going to clean a house, before lifting up furniture and getting into the deep dirt, you would want to see what you are dealing with as a whole. First, you would probably want to examine all the rooms and see what state they were in. Of course, you may discover cobwebs and other things behind the surfaces, but it makes sense to do a reconnaissance mission before you jump in.

That's what you need to do with your chakras. It's possible to work with the entire system but you can also feel what is happening chakra by chakra. With a little sensitivity, imagination and an open mind, you can learn to feel your chakras with your hands and understand what state they are in. You can also draw on your memories of your life experiences at specific ages to help you understand which chakras might need balancing.

In order to feel which chakras need attention, all you need are your hands and a quiet space to lie down. To hear the whisper of the energy in your body, you need to turn the volume down everywhere else. So, switch off your phone and put a 'do not disturb' sign on your bedroom door if you need to.

ACTIVATE YOUR HANDS

First you need to get the sensors working in your hands, so rub your hands together slowly and carefully to stimulate the nerve endings in them. Imagine you are washing your hands in the air to activate your senses, then shake them out until they feel buzzy.

PREPARE YOUR BODY

Lie down on your bed and breathe yourself into a state of deep relaxation: start to breathe in deeply and slowly through your nose and then blow out of your mouth even more slowly.

Do this at least ten times, sinking deeper and deeper into your bed with every exhale. You should start to feel your body become a little more sensitive after breathing in this way, and slightly tinglier. The relaxation should feel as if everything has become a little quieter inside your head.

EXAMINE YOURSELF

1. First place your hand above your crotch, the location of your first chakra, about 5–8 cm (2–3 in) away from your body and see how this feels. You can gently move your hands a little around the area to check whether you notice any difference in another position. Stay there and sense what you feel.

2. Move your hands to the left, right, forwards and backwards around the same area – can you feel anything? Does the air feel heavy or different in any way? Simply observe what you have noticed.

3. Move your hands slowly upwards to the spot between your hips, about 5cm (2in) below your belly button – the location of your second chakra. Do you feel drawn to any particular area? Is there a feeling of being pulled in? Again, notice and observe. You may sense that there is something different – that there is heat, cold or heaviness, or a buzzy, tingly feeling. You will get a sense of where in your body feels heavier or more stuck: it may feel like the air is thick or pulling you in more.

4. Move to the spot about 5cm (2in) above your navel, below your ribs, to your third chakra, and repeat.

5. Move to the centre of your chest, the heart chakra; keep your hands above the centre and repeat.

6. Move to the area in the middle of your throat, your throat chakra, and repeat.

7. Move above your forehead, between your eyebrows to your third eye, and repeat.

8. Simply notice what you feel. Afterwards, you may like to write down what you felt at each stage. Make a note of any chakras that felt particularly heavy, cold, hot, sticky, buzzy or tingly, or where you had a sensation of your hand being pulled in. These sensations can indicate an energy imbalance that needs clearing.

THE SHAKE

When you first examine your chakras, it's likely that you will find that heavy feeling in more than one part of your body – this is normal. Your house might be musty, perhaps because the doors haven't been opened in a while. One way to freshen things up is by shaking, which is the equivalent of opening all the windows and letting a load of air in to blitz it all up.

1. Stand with your legs apart and bend your knees a little.
2. Start by jiggling your legs, then gradually let your entire body begin to jiggle and wobble. It can be hilarious to do this (and also to watch someone else do it)!
3. Shake your hands, your arms, your head, your hair – give yourself a total body shake. Do this for about 3–5 minutes, or as long as you can manage. Now stop and feel the sensations in your body.
4. You will feel a sense of peace and then perhaps subtle movement around your body. Congratulations – you have just got your energy moving and felt your energy flow!

CHAKRA CLEANING MASSAGE

Working with all the chakras in one go, this is a complete chakra meditation and full-body movement exercise to be done standing up.

Put on a song that you love to move to.

Place your hands in the air above your chakra points and move them in an anti-clockwise direction as if you are cleaning them with a cloth, but turn it into a massage movement. Repeat for every chakra. You may feel a sense of lightness as heavy energies are released.

MORNING ENERGY ROUTINE

Are you the kind of person who waits for your mess to build up, or do you like to keep things in check every day? If you have never worked with your energy before, it's likely that a lot of old things may be causing blocks and have built up over the years. I'm sure your mum would have told you to clean your home as you go along – and this is exactly the right way to approach cleaning your energy and your chakras.

A daily practice to keep the chakras moving correctly is the healthiest way to approach this sort of work, and I think that incorporating activities into your daily routine is the simplest way to keep things in check. You can affect your energy even before you leave the house in the morning!

ON WAKING

When you wake up, say to yourself, 'Today is going to be a great day!' This might sound like blind optimism, but it's entirely possible to direct the course of your life by sending out an intention of how you want things to go.

You are literally sending out that vision into the world to pave the way for the possibility of a great day.

THE SNOOZE

1. If you can give yourself a fifteen-minute 'snooze' before getting up, place your hands on your body wherever they feel comfortable.
2. Start breathing nice and slowly, and imagine heat is building up in your hands wherever they are. If they feel like moving, allow them to move as they want to. Enjoy the feeling of the heat going into your body through your hands.
3. If there is something particular you want to happen that day, imagine it happening. This is like a conscious dream – you are awake now, so you can decide what you think about, but you are still in the sleepy zone so you are totally relaxed. The key is to feel the happiness in your body of the thing happening, so picture it happening and how you will feel and react. Smile to yourself: you are dreaming your perfect day. It can be anything from giving a successful presentation to having a good journey to work – it's your dream, so you decide. Top athletes use this technique to secure success; they will picture winning the race well before they compete in it.

BRUSHING YOUR TEETH

When you brush your teeth, look at yourself in the mirror and smile. Your hair may be sticking up and you may have sleep in your eyes – and that's even better. Just smile and laugh at yourself as you would a person you really like. Send a beam of love to yourself in the mirror.

THE MORNING SHOWER

Now it's time to clean your energy! When you jump into the shower and feel the hot water on your head or your neck, imagine that the water is actually a shower of light. It is pouring down on you and washing away any emotional grime that may be bothering you. While you cleanse your outsides, imagine that the water is going through you and cleansing your insides too.

Tip: Do not look at your phone, or turn on the TV or radio until you have got dressed and completed this routine. This is because you need your mind and body to be a blank slate so that they can be receptive. Leave it as long as possible to let the outside world in, because once outside stimuli take over, you will find it's ten times harder to get into the right state of mind.

You can now go about your day, having given yourself the best possible start.

A Lifestyle for Optimum Flow – the Holistic Approach

Working with our chakras is about more than taking certain actions to tackle certain problems. It's a style with which to approach life. In this way of living, we need to be aware of the energy that we are receiving, giving and circulating around our bodies; it's a bit like looking at the surrounding landscape from the top of the hill.

Our mind affects our emotions and our emotions affect our body. There is a direct correlation between what we think and how we feel, how we feel and how we behave, how we behave and what happens in our life. If you want to change your life, then quite simply change how you think. The chakra system will support this process and help you adjust your trajectory to one that benefits you and will help you to have the life you want.

Being your own housekeeper does not mean just showing up once a week to do a bit of tidying. This is a live-in position with full responsibility for the whole building! It requires an awareness at all times of what is going on in you. This may sound daunting, but, like anything, the more you do it, the easier it gets – until such a time that you find you are monitoring your thoughts and emotions without even noticing. This does not mean that you never get angry or upset; far from it. But it does mean that you only get upset for as long as is needed and that you do not dwell or wallow in that place. If you need to be angry, get angry and say or do whatever you need to do, then move through your anger as quickly as possible. It's about flow, feeling your emotions and getting past them. It's not about ignoring or denying them, but allowing, accepting and then gliding through them until calm comes again.

For example, let's say you need to have it out with someone. This would be about communication which correlates to the throat chakra, or, as we suggested, in the fifth-floor creative studio. You may need to make a mess and perhaps get some paints out in the studio to express yourself fully. The paint might go everywhere when you let rip, a Jackson Pollock masterpiece of a row! However, once it's done, you should clean the room and make it good again – don't leave the paint smears on the walls. It's the same situation in real life. Ensure you have cleared the air and have a constructive route forwards with whomever you are arguing. Do not leave any lasting damage.

My approach to chakras is completely holistic. When you see yourself from the highest vantage point, you understand that you are a beautiful, multistorey, rainbow being and you should consider yourself in the full spectrum. You may focus on individual chakras or colours for specific issues and then work through them quickly one by one. However, it's even more encouraging to know that those separate issues are less likely to stick around for long when you are working with the whole system as one.

It's empowering to think that you are actually in charge of everything that happens in your mind and body. If something external happens – a figurative car crash that throws you – how you cope with it is essentially within your control. You can use the energy in your chakra system and your understanding of these principles to put yourself back in the driving seat.

Chakra Clinic

Welcome to the chakra clinic, where you will be given a chakra prescription of different activities that you can do to heal some everyday problems and get your flow back! The chakra clinic is a great place to turn to when you have stresses, strains or emotional issues. Partners, best friends, work, family, relationships – whatever your problem, let's see if we can sort it out here.

The kind of medicine you will be prescribed in this clinic is going to treat your body, mind and soul. We are looking to work holistically to rebalance your chakra system. The natural way to harmonise your chakras is through a fully integrated lifestyle where, as mentioned you are feeling good, eating well, moving your body and achieving something, but there are of course specific practices you can try in specific situations. The prescriptions I offer here include breathwork, healing, meditations and visualisations, as well as physical movements or exercises, foods, baths, crystals and oils.

Meditation

Meditation is simply a way to quieten the mind so that you can rejuvenate – you can think of it as mind discipline training. When we learn to focus at will and find stillness inside ourselves, we can access insights and reach a place of consciousness that will give us freedom from the things that usually bother us.

Meditation exercises are a very effective way to work with the chakras and to rebalance and harmonise the flow in the body. You may find it easier to record the guided steps on your phone in your own voice and play them back to yourself. It really doesn't matter what you sound like, so even if you cringe at the sound of your own voice, remember that only you will hear your recording and it means that you don't have to keep referring back to the book while meditating. It will become your own little tool and you'll remember it more clearly because you made it yourself – you'll become your own personal meditation guru!

Visualisation

Visualisation helps to bring all your chakras into synchronisation and is a form of meditation. It calms the wayward mind so that instead of running wild, it does what you tell it to do. You are essentially training your mind to get out of its own way by giving it something to focus on. Our minds, or the part of the brain concerned with day-to-day living, are often part of the problem, because the noise they create interferes with our focus. Imagine that you are a parent and your mind is your toddler: the child needs entertaining so the parent can get some work done. Giving your mind something to do helps give your body space to heal and your energy some space to rebalance.

Visualisation works in a very peculiar way, because the brain also doesn't know the difference between a real memory and an imagined one – which is extraordinarily useful, especially if you are a bit skint or in a lockdown! So, you can imagine you are on a beach chilling when you are really inside your home, and your brain will send the same happy, relaxed signals to your body as if you really were on a beach and not stuck at home. This means you can trick your brain with visualisation. *Shhh* – don't tell it!

Movement

As you have seen, the chakras relate to different sections of the body and gentle movements can stimulate and work with these points. We aim to bring space to joints and free up the pathways so that energy may flow more freely. The movements I prescribe are simple and based on hatha yoga or gentle stretching. The exercises are meant to feel good for the body, though we should challenge ourselves a little and keeping pushing our edge of what is comfortable.

Note: It goes without saying that you must check with a medical professional if you are pregnant, have an injury, feel pain, or are in any way unsure about doing these exercises.

Energy Healing

This is an amazing phenomenon that you really have to try in order to believe. Exercises for energy healing involve breathing while focusing on your palms to generate heat and energy (which are then reapplied to your own body in the exercises below). The way to generate this energy is to begin breathing in and out while picturing your breath going down your arms and into your hands. You may have to use your imagination to get the breath energy flowing into your palms at first, but after a short while it will actually start to happen.

Once the energy is in your hands, direct it intuitively into your body; your body will understand and draw it in where it is needed. It's an inherent language that we all speak, but which we may have forgotten. When you try healing, it may at first feel distant yet also familiar, because the ability was always there.

Crystals

Crystals and crystal energy can be a great way to support your chakra health. Crystals hold unique frequencies and correspond to different chakras. Quartz has been proven to give off an electrical charge known as piezoelectricity. Through the process of entrainment, whereby one object aligns with the higher vibration of the other, the vibration of the crystal will align with the vibration of the chakra and bring it into balance.

Essential Oils

These are oils captured from the essence of a plant or flower. Through a process of distillation, the vibration of the plant or flower can be contained as an oil. This means that not only can you can access the scent of the flower or plant, you can also connect with its attributes through the concentrated oil. The essential oil is usually added to a carrier oil of some description, such as almond oil; it's rarely used neat. Essential oils have varying frequencies and can align with those of the chakras, depending on what you need.

Note: If you have any physical or psychological symptoms, please be aware that essential oils and other holistic treatments are not alternatives to consulting a qualified medical doctor, but options that can be used to complement whatever other treatments you may be receiving.

For Calm

Problem: Anxiety and Stress

When our bodies believe there is a threat, we activate a defence system that is intended to give us the means to get rid of it. In response the threat, our bodies use all our resources at once to stand up to it, run away from it or pretend we are dead; in other words, fight, flight or freeze. Anxiety can trigger a full spectrum of responses, but a common thread that my clients report is a feeling of losing control. That feeling of vulnerability or fear, when it comes, is like an old wound opening up again. Whatever the reason for the anxiety, whether the threat is real or perceived, our bodies will jump into action to deal with it.

HOW DOES THIS AFFECT THE CHAKRAS AND ENERGY FLOW?

From small jitters to a full-blown panic attack, stress and anxiety will impact the entire chakra system. These emotional states can affect our first chakra with fear, which stops us in our tracks; and they can also affect our second chakra in our lower stomach, giving rise to digestive disorders, which may then affect our third chakra and prevent us from being able to do anything. Our upper chakras will shut down completely, so our heart chakra will close down – as will our throats – making it impossible to think or speak clearly. Anxiety and stress in our lower chakras quite literally stops the flow of energy to the sixth chakra completely and our whole system says, 'No!' The only way to deal with it is to work with the entire body to remove the state of stress and restore a natural state.

So, when you feel anxiety mounting, here are some things you can do …

PRESCRIPTION

THE SEDATIVE

When anxiety begins to spiral, it can take you by surprise and you may not have time to get external help. This hack can be done instantly, the minute your heart starts racing and you get that awful feeling of dread.

1. Rub your hands together until they get hot.
2. Place a hand on the area of your thymus gland (the point above your chest and below your neck).
3. Breathe deeply in through your nose for a count of four.
4. Breathe out slowly through your mouth, as though you were blowing a kiss.
5. Imagine the breath is going into your palm and feel it get hotter.
6. Repeat at least ten times, or until the anxiety subsides.
7. Try to increase the length of the exhale as you progress – for example, a count of five, followed by a count of six, etc. – so that it becomes longer than the inhale.

BOX BREATHING

This is an ancient pranayama or breathing technique designed to reduce anxiety and improve your ability to concentrate. It can be used in any moment of tension or stress, or simply to wind down before bed. It regulates your nervous system, which will help you to focus.

'Box breathing' is so called because your breathing mimics a box shape.

1. Imagine drawing the sides of a box with every four counts of breath.
2. Breathe in through your nose, deeply into your lower belly to relax any tightness you may feel there, and then hold.
3. Breathe out slowly through your mouth as though you are blowing a kiss, then hold.
4. Use this rhythm:

   · Breathing in for a count of four.
   · Holding in for a count of four.
   · Breathing out for a count of four.
   · Holding out for a count of four.

5. Repeat for as long as you need to feel calm again. I recommend setting yourself a timer for at least 5 minutes and then increase the amount of time as your ability to concentrate improves.

TALK TO THE PAGE

When you have a lot of things running through your head, it can feel overwhelming. This is when 'talking to the page' – which simply means writing down whatever you want to get off your chest – can be truly therapeutic. It's a private exercise that will bring calm to your thoughts. If you can make a journaling practice part of your regular routine, this will have a very positive effect on your state of mind.

1. Begin by bringing your awareness to the present moment. Feel your hand and the pen; look down at the page.
2. Write down something you can see, something you can feel, something you can hear, something you can smell and something you can taste.
3. Now start to write down your concerns. Get those troublesome thoughts out of your body and onto the page.

WORRY BOX

The quicker version of 'Talk to the page' is to create a worry box. Worrying is a major energy drain because, by itself, worry is futile – it really doesn't do anything except stress you out.

Write your worry on a piece of paper and pop it in a box. Once it's in the worry box, it's out of your head.

If you can do anything about the issue, put your energy into implementing a solution. If you can't, it just stays in the box and you can then put your energy into feeling better.

HAPPY BOX

This is the opposite of the 'Worry box' exercise. Here, you make a note about something that makes you feel happy or grateful, and then put that in a special box so you can reread your happy notes any time you need an injection of positivity.

For Energy

Problem: Feeling Flat

Sometimes we feel a bit rubbish. There may or may not be a reason, it's just the rhythm of life. It could be a mood that has been looming, or because you feel powerless at the news of what's happening in the world, or it could be related to your hormones. Whatever the cause, it's worth addressing when you notice that you are feeling 'meh'. The solution to feeling flat is no different to any sort of device that may be running out of juice – your battery needs charging.

HOW DOES THIS AFFECT THE CHAKRAS AND ENERGY FLOW?

As we have established, we are energy beings and how we feel depends on how our energy is moving through our systems. Feeling depleted is a general feeling that relates to the overall flow in our body and the whole chakra system. If energy is not moving well, we feel sluggish and slow, but there are some instant energy pick-me-ups that you can practise to stimulate the flow and boost the energy in your body. Try these to perk yourself back up again.

PRESCRIPTION

NECKLACE TAPPING

This is exactly what it says on the tin: in this practice, you use your fingers to gently but firmly tap your body to wake up specific energy points and get your energy moving again. Sometimes when I've been working with clients, I'll need a wake-up afterwards – and tapping in the shape of a necklace seems to do the trick: I feel invigorated and energised after this process.

1. Beginning on one shoulder, tap with your fingers in the shape of a necklace, going down to the thymus point and then back up to the other shoulder; then back over to the opposite side again.
2. Tap like this over the top area of your back as well. Repeat this process three or four times on both sides of your body.
3. Swap hands and repeat in the opposite direction on both sides of your body at least three or four times.

Tip: Use as much pressure as feels invigorating without bruising yourself.

LIGHT SHOWER

This is the equivalent of plugging into the light of the universe and charging yourself up from the inside out.

1. Sit quietly and takes some deep, long breaths, allowing your focus to go inward.
2. Try to find a place of stillness inside yourself.
3. Now imagine that a beam of beautiful, warm and powerful light is coming down from the sky.
4. It is coming down directly on to you and all around you – and it starts to flood you with feelings of safety and love.

5. Imagine this light is filling you up as though you were an empty vase and see yourself lighting up from within, shining like a glow worm.
6. When you are fully lit, remain in the feeling for a few minutes.
7. Complete the process by rubbing your hands together and pressing your hands on opposite shoulders to anchor the feeling.

THE SHAKE

We looked at 'The shake' earlier, when taking stock of our energy system. Shaking is also what animals do in the wild to let go of trauma. The action activates the parasympathetic nervous system and refreshes the body's energy flow – great for when you need a boost. See page 62 and repeat the steps given there.

Problem: Feeling Drained

Some people or situations can suck the life out of you. After a difficult conversation, moment of upset or annoying interaction with someone, you can be left feeling empty. We all know people who complain a lot, and even after they have gone, we can feel as though we are now carrying their worries. This is because we may have taken on the burdensome energy of their negativity without realising it. Sometimes people will leave their heavy energy and take your light, happy energy instead. They will go home feeling better, having let off steam, while you are left feeling depleted and dreadful.

HOW DOES THIS AFFECT THE CHAKRAS AND ENERGY FLOW?

The energy you have either lost or gained after a heavy interaction will affect your entire system. Sometimes this sort of unhealthy, draining connection can continue through into your thoughts as well! You will need to clean yourself energetically and rid yourself of the 'feeling' – or literally cut off the source of the negativity.

PRESCRIPTION

THE CLEANSE AND RESET

This exercise brushes the energetic residue off and away from you, and removes the energetically challenging connection with the person, place or thing.

1. Sweep your body with your hands down in a diagonal direction from shoulder to hip on each side.
2. Brush down your arms and the fronts of your legs.
3. Repeat with vigour until you feel energetically clean again.
4. When you are done, stand up strong with your shoulders back and thump your chest like Tarzan!

Tip: Make a noise if you can - you will feel better from the invigorating energy that has been activated by making this sound, especially if you are laughing at yourself.

BRUSHING SALT BATH

Bathing in Epsom salts and magnesium flakes is another wonderful way to cleanse yourself of heavy energies.

1. Fill your bath with hot water to your preferred temperature and add at least a cup or two of magnesium flakes and of Epsom salts – be generous.
2. Before you step in, set an intention and ask out loud that the water wash away any heaviness from your day.

3. Use a body brush to brush your skin downwards, as this will brush off the residue of the interaction. You can also use your hand if you do not have a brush.
4. Dunk your head and imagine that when you emerge you will be fresh and cleansed from the heaviness.

For Happiness

Problem: Feeling Down

Unhappiness can creep in when we are unsatisfied in some way, perhaps because our expectations haven't been met or things aren't going the way we wanted, but it can often be because we feel alienated from ourselves or other people. The truth is a lot of our discontent can arise because we have become disconnected from life and nature. We have been hanging out in a dreary place in our heads for too long and we need some love.

HOW DOES THIS AFFECT THE CHAKRAS AND ENERGY FLOW?

Happiness is chakra food – it boosts our energy. Unhappiness quite literally drains our entire chakra system and we lose our flow. Irrespective of what the catalyst was for our sour mood, we can switch out of it again so easily by using nature as a tool. The sooner we reconnect, the quicker we can restore our energy flow.

PRESCRIPTION

WALK IN NATURE

An easy way to feel better is to find a park or green space and go for a simple walk in nature. In recent times this has been called 'earthing', but it's as simple as turning off your phone, putting one foot in front of another and enjoying the trees, grass and whatever other scenery you see. Happiness often comes from appreciating beauty, so when you walk, try to notice the small, pretty things that you might encounter. Notice how each tree is perfect in its bark and leaves; notice the colours of the leaves or any birds that you see. The act of simply slowing down and being aware of the beauty all around you will bring happiness to your being without you even realising it.

GROUNDING

Sometimes, if you have been spending too much time in your head and feeling upset, you will need to come back down to earth by spending some time grounding yourself. A very simple way to do this is to actually touch nature.

Touch a tree

You can hug a tree, but if you feel self-conscious, simply lean your back against a tree, stand on its roots if you can and feel the tree supporting you. Silently ask for the tree's energy to enter into your back and see if you can feel anything – it might be a vibration or a buzz, or another gentle sensation coming through you. You'll be surprised by how easy it is to feel a tree.

Touch the earth

Feeling the earth on the soles of your feet is another step towards feeling better, so walk barefoot on the ground. If you can take your shoes off and walk, this is going to give you an enhanced feeling of well-being and make you feel connected to the earth.

Grow roots

Sitting or standing quietly on the earth, take nine very deep, long, slow breaths and feel yourself become still. Imagine that roots are growing out of your tailbone or your feet: picture them growing down into the earth, and down to the depths of the earth. They are spreading out and locking you into the soil. Feel secure and held by these roots and become aware of a sense of safety coming back up through the roots into your being. Let that feeling make its way all the way through you, helping you to relax inside.

DANCE

It's impossible to feel unhappy when you are dancing to music you like – trust me, I've tried! Dancing releases endorphins that make you happy. Put on the music you love, close the door and curtains if necessary, and dance like no one is watching – because no one is. You are guaranteed to feel better after a boogie!

For Confidence

Problem: Feeling Indecisive

When we have a big decision to make, it can be nerve-racking, especially if we don't have a clear sense of direction. We may be torn in many different ways, not only through our own needs, but balancing those of others who may be affected. Finding clarity and strength to stand behind our views is what's needed to move forwards.

HOW DOES THIS AFFECT THE CHAKRAS AND ENERGY FLOW?

If we lack a sense of self with respect to what is right for us, indecision can be felt in the sacral chakra in the lower stomach. If we are afraid of what we truly desire, indecision can be felt in the heart chakra. If we are overthinking the situation and possible outcomes, it can be felt in the third eye chakra.

By clearing and working with these three chakras, we can see through the fog of indecision and look to these chakras once more to help us to work out what to do. Activating our third eye chakra can also aid us by reconnecting us to our intuition and inner sense of knowing.

PRESCRIPTION

ASK YOUR BODY

We can often sense things in our gut. In fact, it's no coincidence that the gut is called the second brain, because it sends signals to the brain about the stimulus it's receiving. This is why people with anxiety often suffer from digestive issues.

1. Think of one option in your decision. Now, take your awareness into your stomach and rest it there. Try to tune in to how you feel here – are you tense, jittery or relaxed?
2. Move into your heart area: how does your chest feel in response to this option? Is it open, closed or tight? The heart's voice is usually quieter but more consistent.
3. Now move into your mind: what does it say? It has probably run through a million scenarios already and might be shouting at you.
4. If you feel relaxed yet excited in your stomach, your heart feels light and you have butterflies up high (in a good, energised way), this means that your stomach, heart and head are all in agreement about the potential benefits of this option.
5. If you feel heavy, anxious and drained, their response is a 'no' or a 'not sure' – so it's best to wait to make your decision. Often, it takes time for the right course of action to become clear, when the whole body is in agreement. If you cannot wait, go with what your heart is saying because the heart doesn't operate from the perspective of the ego.

INNER KNOWING CHANT

You can also ask your intuition or your sixth chakra to help you by activating the third eye. 'Om' is the sound of the universe and it will help you to get clarity inside your mind's eye.

1. Breathe deeply, inhaling and exhaling nine times.
2. Chant the word *om*, but make the sound long and drawn out: *AAAAAUUUUUUUMMMMMMMMMMMM*.
3. Feel the vibrations in your body and try to focus on the spot between your eyebrows.
4. Repeat at least nine times.
5. You can increase the number of repetitions with practice, stopping when you feel it's the right time.

Tip: Before you go to sleep, ask out loud to be given guidance to help you know what to do. Then, in the morning, immediately make notes on your dreams and see what come through. Guidance can also come in the form of clues in the dreaming or waking hours – for example, something someone says, a podcast or a meme on Instagram – so be alert and notice what's around you; you may find your *aha!* moment comes at random.

Problem: Can't Be Bothered

When we know what we want to do, we can take action. But sometimes we just don't have the will to get going. These are the times when we can't be bothered and would rather watch TV. This is not to say that you should never be in this zone, but when you really need to complete a task and a deadline is looming, then the TV must be switched off and replaced with some get-up-and-go.

HOW DOES THIS AFFECT THE CHAKRAS AND ENERGY FLOW?

Any sort of energy for action will come from the upper stomach – the site of our third chakra. If we feel tired and unmotivated, the chances are that the blocks will be in our solar plexus and we will need to generate some fire back in our belly.

PRESCRIPTION

BREATH OF FIRE

This is an ancient yogic technique that builds up energy in your stomach and fires you up for the day. It's best done in the morning on an empty stomach before breakfast.

1. Begin by breathing in and out nine times.
2. Take a deep breath in through your nose.
3. Exhale forcefully through your nose and feel your stomach contract in a pumping action.

4. Repeat slowly but build up speed, and continue for 1–5 minutes, or for as long as you can handle.

Tip: Keep your attention and accent on the out-breath; the in-breath will happen without you trying.

FLAME MEDITATION

Fire is the element related to the solar plexus and, by gazing at a flame, you are connecting to that element within you. This is a really easy meditation to do – try it at night when you are winding down.

1. Light a candle.
2. Gaze at the flame.
3. Watch the flame flicker and dance.
4. Soften your focus and allow yourself to get lost in the fire.
5. Notice the colours, the changes and the movement of the flame.
6. Stay there for as long as feels right for you – even 3–5 minutes will be beneficial.

MOVING FORWARDS

As simple as it sounds, you can use your legs to help you to move forwards. Jogging and power walking are excellent actions to get the right energy going to help blitz your apathy. Stomach crunches and cat stretches are also great for this area, because the contractions and then stretches build strength and suppleness in this chakra.

Crunches involve lying on your back with your knees bent and your feet on the floor. Place your hands behind your head and raise your head and torso towards your knees. Repeat at least ten times.

Cat stretches are where you are on your hands and knees, with your shoulders directly above your hands. Alternate between arching and then curving your back, allowing your head to move in line with your spine. Repeat ten times.

SOLAR PLEXUS SCENTS

I like to use a diffuser in which essential oils are dropped into heated water, thereby releasing the fragrance into the air. You could also add a couple of drops of essential oil to a bath for a very vibrant bathing experience – and you can even cook with the herbs themselves! The scent of cooking with them in the kitchen will also have an effect on your third chakra.

Use these essential oil fragrances in your home to clear and stimulate the energy of the solar plexus chakra:

- coriander,
- black pepper,
- cardamom,
- lime,
- juniper.

These scents are known to support the third chakra and help its energy align with an optimum flow.

Problem: Existential Crisis

Sometimes, when we are at our wits' end and we feel lost, life can get on top of us. We might be unsure about who we really are and what our purpose is; and those moments can make us feel confused, depressed and abandoned.

HOW DOES THIS AFFECT THE CHAKRAS AND ENERGY FLOW?

Feeling lost may relate to your crown chakra. If we feel isolated or alone, it's often because we have lost our sense of connection to the universe. We need reminding of our place, that we count and that we are truly a part of something much bigger. We may feel like a single drop of water in these moments of crisis, but we are part of an ocean – and remembering this can be a comfort.

PRESCRIPTION

UNIVERSE MEDITATION

This exercise aims to help you connect with the universe and experience that feeling of oneness. You will understand that you are pure consciousness living in human form. Whether you have a body or not, you would still exist as consciousness. Deep, huh? Try it.

1. Find a comfortable position, such as sitting on a chair or cross-legged with a pillow under you for comfort if you need it.

2. Place the back of your hands on your lap, with thumbs and first fingers touching.
3. Take a deep breath in, breathing down into your lower belly and imagining the air travelling down.
4. Now exhale and imagine the breath coming all the way back up again. Do this twenty-seven times.
5. In time with each in- and out-breath, say in your mind: 'I am consciousness, I am the universe, I am everything.'
6. Start to focus on the fuzzy feeling that you get around your body, where you can't quite work out where you begin and end. This is the feeling of consciousness.
7. Every time your mind wanders off, simply say, 'I am the universe', then bring it back and start again. It doesn't matter how many times you need to do this.

For Work

Problem: Confidence at Work

At work, our confidence can often take a battering and we may be ridden with feelings of fear and insecurity. This could be because of a meeting that went badly, a decision that has not gone our way, a difficult encounter with our manager or even because of the loss of our job. Whatever the reason, we need to recover our sense of purpose so that we can take the best course of action. Your state of energy and your attitude will determine how the loss plays out. Whatever it is, it's time to dream of an even better future.

Remember that when one door closes, usually a better one will open – even if you can't immediately see it. It may not have been an option previously, but you are now being invited to re-examine what you do and how you do it. Life sometimes deals us cards like this so that we can move into something that is even better aligned with our true selves.

HOW DOES THIS AFFECT THE CHAKRAS AND ENERGY FLOW?

Our first chakra is likely to be affected in a situation like this, because we will worry about whether we can fulfil our potential and even survive and provide for ourselves and those who depend on us. It may also affect our second chakra if we identify strongly with the role we now feel insecure in, or which we have just lost, so we may find ourselves wondering who we are. It will also affect our fifth and sixth chakras, because the energy of the lower ones means we will likely be ruminating heavily about loss and perhaps what we could have said or done differently, and so forth.

With the following exercises, you will stimulate your root chakra to strengthen that area and the energy running through your foundations.

PRESCRIPTION

MOVE AND STRETCH YOUR ROOT

This is a grounding exercise that brings you back into your body – ideal if you have been living too much in your head. It also helps to make you feel safe and secure by activating the earthy energy of the root chakra.

1. Massage your first chakra by lying on your back and hugging your knees into your chest. You can rock a little or do one knee at a time. Stay in this position for thirty seconds to one minute, or as long as is comfortable for you.
2. Alternate this with a bridge pose. Lie on your back, put your feet on the ground, bend your knees and lift your pelvis and back off the floor to stretch and activate your lowest chakra. Stay in this position for thirty seconds to one minute, or as long as is comfortable.
3. Now sit on a chair, or on the ground, and rock your pelvis forwards and backwards to stimulate the root chakra. Stay in this position for thirty seconds to one minute, or as long as is comfortable.

Tip: Burn some sandalwood incense or oil. This scent will help to connect you with your first chakra if you are feeling worried about lack and spiralling loss, and the fragrance will help bring you back down to earth.

THE DAILY GRATITUDE LOG

Gratitude is an extremely high vibrational energy and by installing this in your body regularly, you raise your frequency dramatically, which will help you to get through upsetting situations.

1. Before going to bed, think about everything that is going well in your life.
2. List all the things that you are truly thankful for and focus on them.
3. Write them down in a little notepad.

Tip: Be sure to do this exercise every day for at least twenty-one days, but ideally forever!

MANIFEST A NEW SITUATION

There is a trick to manifesting that very few people know. In order to attract something into your life, you have to pretend you already have it. So, if you want a great new job, for example, you should spend time regularly every day imagining that you have secured a new position, your dream job, and that you are already there, learning, being challenged, making friends and loving it. Essentially you need to wallow in the feelings of *already having the thing you want*.

Our brains may want to wait for the thing to show up before we enjoy the feeling of it, but, frustratingly, that's not how the Law of Attraction works. We have to become the energy of what we want and believe and trust that it's coming in order to reel it into our lives.

As you settle down to sleep, imagine you are happy and content in a new situation. (Even if you aren't sure exactly what it should be, focus on the feeling.)

Smile as you go to sleep in the knowledge that it's coming.

Feel reassured that the more you do this, the closer and quicker it will come. Life will figure out the details. Be open to any insights and help that might start coming your way.

SOOTHING TIRED HEAD AND EYES

Palming is a technique that works on your mind to relieve overthinking and headaches. It soothes the sixth chakra and calms an overactive mind. If you have been staring at a screen all day, this is an easy energy hack that can revitalise you.

1. Shake your hands vigorously, then rub them together and place them in a prayer position.
2. Now imagine that your deep in-breaths are travelling into your palms; wait for your palms to feel buzzy.
3. Place your palms on your eyes, like a child playing hide and seek.
4. Stay there and allow the heat energy to move into your eyelids. You should find that after a short while your eyes feel better.

For
Relationships

Problem: Heartbreak

The grief from the loss of love is very real and no one is immune to it. When we are suffering from the pain of a broken heart, it's hard to focus on anything else. Depending on what happened, the experience may affect our ability to trust or be vulnerable with others, and we may feel anger, regret, deep sadness and grief.

HOW DOES THIS AFFECT THE CHAKRAS AND ENERGY FLOW?

Broken hearts often quite literally relate to the heart chakra. Grief is a tangible emotion and we can feel actual physical pain in our heart muscle. This chakra is very sensitive and can shut down easily. The healing in this particular area will take time and cannot be rushed, but gently reminding the heart that it is safe once more is a good way to start.

Heartbreak can also encompass other complex feelings that may be linked to other chakras as well, especially if hurt and betrayal were a part of the story.

Here follows a comprehensive technique to help encourage the heart and any other affected chakra to open up again and be healed. I recommend recording the instructions first so that you can listen to them while you follow the steps.

PRESCRIPTION

GRIEF RELIEF HEALING EXERCISE

It's a lot easier to work with the energy of grief when you have turned it into a physical presence and located it in your body. This exercise aims to find and help soothe it in a way that feels real. Of course healing grief takes time, but it's very powerful to be able to actually 'see' your pain decrease.

Relax:

1. Lie down somewhere quiet where you won't be disturbed and close your eyes. Get yourself into a relaxed state by breathing deeply in through your nose for a count of four and out even slower through your mouth for a count of eight. Purse your lips and blow slowly in an elongated fashion to slow down the out-breath. Do this at least nine times or until you feel significantly more relaxed. Keep breathing in this circular pattern.

Identify the pain:

2. Now think about the pain you are feeling. Where is it in your body? Which chakra is it nearest to? It might not be the heart, so go with whatever your instincts tell you.
3. How does it feel? Try to make it into a shape – does it have a colour or a texture? How big is it? What is it made out of? Let whatever comes into your mind be the answer; there is no right or wrong.

4. How intense does it feel on a scale of one to ten, if one is barely there and ten is excruciating and unbearable?
5. Now you have made the pain into a three-dimensional object and you can feel it in one of your chakras.

Clean the chakra:

6. Next, put your fingers on your preferred hand together; this is going to create your 'stirring stick'. Imagine you are dropping your hand directly into the nearest chakra that the pain is coming from and move your hand in an anti-clockwise direction round and round about ten to twelve times, as if you were stirring a pot.
7. Now stop. Rest and breathe deeply. Imagine you are breathing into the chakra, into the shape of the pain. Use your breath to break it up and dissolve it.
8. Has it changed? Has the intensity decreased on a scale of one to ten? Make a note of any differences.
9. Repeat the whole process at least three to five times, or as many times as needed until the shape starts to soften, diminish or even disappear.

Boost the chakra:

10. Imagine a beautiful beam of light coming down from the sky directly into the chakra, filling it up. Breathe in deeply and imagine this light is flooding into your chakra. Feel the warmth of this happening in your mind.

11. Now drop your hand in once more and circle around clockwise. Then place your hand on your skin to lock in the feeling. When you feel full, light and charged, open your eyes.

QUICK HEART CHAKRA BOOSTER

If you want to give your heart some extra healing, try this short and sweet addition to the 'Grief relief healing' exercise. '*Yam*' is a sacred sound or mantra that stimulates the heart chakra with its unique vibration.

Allow the beam of light to move into your heart chakra, if it wasn't already there, and open yourself up to receive.

Chant the word – *YAAAAAAAAAM* – and feel this word in your heart as the light enters your heart and fills you up.

Problem: A Break-up

A break-up is never easy, irrespective of whose decision it was. Aside from healing the heart, there may also be practical living arrangements to reorganise, children, pets, friends, a whole life to carve up somehow – it can be a totally disorientating time.

HOW DOES THIS AFFECT THE CHAKRAS AND ENERGY FLOW?

The chakras affected by a break-up could be any or all of the chakras in our system. How secure we feel, our self-esteem, our motivation, our ability to relate and to speak out, as well our ability to trust our intuition, have all been put through a mangle. We may feel as though we have been split into pieces that need to be glued back together.

We may miss many things about our old life with that person and one of the main things we may miss is the feeling of their physical affection. This can be addressed in the exercises below.

PRESCRIPTION

ME HUG

Touch is an important part of self-care and getting you back into a flow feeling, and there is no reason why you should do without it. If you have little children or pets, you can give them hugs, but whatever is going on in your life –

even a global pandemic – 'me hugs' are always ready and waiting for you.

Place your hands across yourself, close your eyes and hold your arms. Take a deep breath and imagine you are your own friend and you are hugging yourself. Feel the warmth and love coming from you to yourself. Imagine you are your best friend, giving you a genuine and tender hug.

HEALING THE HEART

This is a version of the Buddhist meditation called Metta Bhavana, also known as loving-kindness, which centres on sending love to ourselves and then outwards to others.

1. Begin by being quiet – take some long, deep, slow breaths to find a place of stillness.
2. Think of your heart. Feel your heart inside your chest and concentrate on the sensation of your heart. Imagine sending pink heart energy to yourself from inside yourself.
3. Now picture someone you love and send loving heart energy from you to them.
4. Think of the world and repeat.

HEART ENERGY

There is a reason why roses are traditionally given to lovers. Not only do they smell divine but their oil has one of the highest vibrational frequencies of all flowers and it is aligned to the heart chakra. It's no surprise, then, that the crystal vibration of rose quartz works wonders for this area too and that you can use this crystal as well as rose oil to help you to heal your heart. Their comforting presence will encourage you to soften so you can love yourself and 'be' in the heavenly, high vibration of love.

Carry a piece of rose quartz in your pocket, or, even better, close to the skin, near to your heart chakra. If you wear a bra, place it in there. A rose quartz pendant of the right length is also ideal.

To enjoy the support of rose oil, you will need:

a few drops of pure rose oil
1 tsp carrier oil, such as almond oil

1. Add the drops of rose oil to your carrier oil.
2. Anoint your heart chakra and your pulse points with the oils.

Problem: Lost Your Mojo

Sometimes in life we can lose our feeling of creativity or our libido and feel totally uninspired. However, there are some things we can do to get that feeling flowing again. Creative and sexual energy are actually the same thing, so when we get one going, we automatically kick-start the other.

HOW DOES THIS AFFECT THE CHAKRAS AND ENERGY FLOW?

These feelings can relate to our sacral chakra and whether we are moving energy through this area in a healthy way. The following activities are all designed to reactivate and ignite this area by encouraging the energy of the sacral chakra to flow.

PRESCRIPTION

SACRED SACRAL BATH RITUAL

This sequence of activities is designed to get you inspired and feeling juicy again. Any of the parts can be done separately or together for maximum effect. Find an hour or so, make sure you will not be disturbed and settle into the ritual.

Part 1: Prepare to awaken

You will need:

approx. 15 drops of neroli essential oil
approx. 15 drops of ylang-ylang essential oil
rose petals or rose essential oil (or both)
foamy soap or body cleansing gel

1. Run a hot bath and add the neroli and ylang-ylang oils – you need to be able to smell them easily.
2. If you have some dried rose petals, put a handful of those in as well and/or add a few drops of rose oil.
3. Before getting into the bath, state out loud to the water your intention to: 'Wash away any blocks affecting my creativity or sexuality.' Step into the bath, lie back and dip your head in the water for a moment or two.
4. Focus on the sensation of water on your skin and tune in to how it feels. Allow the water to lap all around you and enjoy the feeling.
5. Sensuously massage yourself with a foamy shower gel or soap – use touch to stimulate your skin, inhale the scent of the oils and feel it go inside your lungs.

Part 2: Be your own lover

You will need:

5-10 drops of each of your choice of floral essential oils approx. 50ml/2fl oz body moisturiser or carrier oil

1. Add the drops of essential oil to the moisturiser or carrier oil.
2. After your bath, apply the moisturiser or oil to your whole body.
3. The secret to this is to massage yourself the way you would want a lover to do it. Just how *you* like it – take your time. The aim here is to activate your senses and restore the flow of energy.

Part 3: Stimulate the second chakra

Pelvic stretches:

1. Once you are clean and moisturised, put on something super comfy.
2. Lie on your back with your knees bent and the soles of your feet pressed together. Let your legs fall apart to the sides.
3. Stay there for at least five minutes, breathing deeply in and out.
4. Imagine you are breathing in the colour orange into your pelvic area, before breathing it out again.

Hip circles and sexy strutting:

1. Stand with your feet apart and your hands on your hips.
2. Circle clockwise with your hips and then anti-clockwise – really get your pelvic area moving. Close your eyes and lose yourself in the movement.
3. Now walk forwards as if you were parading down a catwalk. I'm talking completely over-the-top sexy strutting. Walk back again.
4. This is about loosening up, reigniting your mojo and feeling sassy again, so even if it seems silly, remember that no one else is watching you.

Tip: Ensure you have privacy for this ritual. It's important that you can feel safe and undisturbed to be able to truly relax into this self-care.

Problem: The Difficult Conversation

Are there some chats that you dread – for instance, in an uncomfortable work situation or about an icky subject with someone close? You may be worried about their reaction or about your own response, especially if emotions are involved. If you don't like confrontation, the mere thought of open and honest conversations about awkward subjects can be excruciating.

HOW DOES THIS AFFECT THE CHAKRAS AND ENERGY FLOW?

This situation relates back to our throat chakra, where we speak our truth. If we feel fearful of speaking, this can create a ball of heavy energy, usually situated in the neck, and we can develop a block in our throat chakra. Clearing the block will help us to feel that we can say what we need to say.

PRESCRIPTION

HUMMING

Humming is a fun and effective way to activate and clear a chakra – I particularly love this technique. The word '*ham*' is a sacred sound or mantra. Its special vibration activates the throat chakra, and it feels so good to do.

1. Get quiet and take some deep breaths in and out to enter a still place. (You might like to do this in a private place!)

2. Begin humming. Try to feel the hum reverberating in your throat.
3. After you have got this going, start humming the word '*ham*' but draw it out: *HAAAAAAAMMMMMMM*.
4. Repeat at least twelve times. If you can do more, then do!

HIGHER SELF CHAT

If you can't talk to the person easily, try talking first to their Higher Self. Their Higher Self is the name given to the wise part of them where the ego isn't involved. You can access their Higher Self through a meditation that takes you to the higher realms.

1. Breathe yourself deeply into a place of relaxation.
2. Imagine you are in a place in nature.
3. Find a tree you like the look of and imagine climbing effortlessly up it.
4. When you get to the top, keep going up into the sky, into the clouds, higher and higher until you can't go any further.
5. Ask to speak to the Higher Self of the person in question and wait for them to arrive. Sometimes their Higher Self might look like a big ball of energy; just be open to whatever comes.
6. Send their Higher Self love, and tell them that you want what's best for everyone and you are coming from a decent place. Tell them that you do not want to hurt them and wish them only goodness.

7. When you have finished, thank them, embrace them and make your way back down the way you came.
8. Feel confident that on some level of consciousness the person will have received your peace communication.

Tip: Do whatever feels right, but remember you don't need to get into the nitty gritty of the issue with a Higher Self; this is about clearing the energy pathway for a conversation to flow easily with your lower selves in real life.

To Get Well Soon

Problem: Aches

While you should always consult a medical professional for any major health concerns, healing with energy is my go-to treatment for any sort of minor pain. Even if you aren't a trained healer, you can comfort yourself using just your hands and your breath. The beauty of this technique is that it can be used anywhere for anything, whether it's tackling period pain at work, soothing a headache or simply in a moment when you need some TLC – energy healing works for any sort of discomfort. The energy that you apply to yourself will hit the spot and soothe whatever is needed at that moment.

HOW DOES THIS AFFECT THE CHAKRAS AND ENERGY FLOW?

Illness can often be the physical consequence of an untreated energy block. The pain will be connected to the zone of the particular chakra that corresponds to the area of the body in question and its associated emotions. When something hurts, our mind will be preoccupied and the energy flow of the whole body will be affected. Energy healing will first help to relieve the discomfort, so that the body can relax once more, and then allow the healing to penetrate further in order to work on the original cause of the block.

Here is a very simple guide to doing your own healing, whatever the ailment.

PRESCRIPTION

ENERGY HEALING – FOR ALL MINOR AILMENTS

If you are feeling out of sorts, you can alleviate any kind of ache with energy healing. It offers a gradual kind of relief, which reaches the source of the pain and restores the flow of energy in the body. It's gentle, comforting and connects you with your body.

Note: Energy healing is *not* an alternative to medical care – it is a complementary technique. You must continue with any course of treatment that your doctor has prescribed.

Get quiet:

Find a private space; if you aren't at home, even a toilet cubicle will work. Get quiet inside by using long, deep breaths – in through the nose and then blowing out in a gentle, drawn-out way with your lips slightly pursed.

Activate your hands:

Hold your hands in a prayer position. Begin by rubbing your hands together until they feel hot and tingly. Focus on your palms and start to direct the long breath into them, using your imagination. After a while your hands should activate and start to feel hot. This can take a few minutes.

Apply the energy:

Rest your hands on your body and tune in to where the ache is coming from. Then let your hands move to the spot where it hurts. Allow the heat to enter you through your hands. If you need to increase the sensation, continue to focus your breath into your palms.

Tip: This is an intuitive practice and requires patience. Allow your hand to rest in one position for as long as you can, as sometimes it can take a while to feel the effects. Your body will direct your hands to where it wants them to go and when you find a spot that feels good, just relax in that place to allow the energy to penetrate. Give plenty of time to that position.

PERIOD PAIN RELIEVER

Period pain or any sort of stomach cramp can be awful. In the same way that heat can help, we can use energy to have a similar effect. This is particularly helpful for treating stomach cramps that affect the sacral chakra area and perhaps our mind too if the pain is distracting.

Simply use the energy healing technique described above and breathe into the hurting area through your hands. The trick is to allow your breath to create energy in your hands until they get hot. It's your own personal, portable hot water bottle and should provide some instant relief. It can even be done at your desk if you are at work!

HEADACHE

Headaches can be soothed away with the same energy healing technique as period pain, but by placing your hands on your temples or forehead and cheeks. While you are doing your healing, apply a small amount of pressure. You can also gently massage the sides of your head if it feels good.

Final Words

Looking after the health of your chakras is an everyday awareness activity that involves your mind, your body and your soul. It's holistic in the sense that it involves you as a whole – every moment, every day, all of you. When you commit to working with your chakras, you will gradually become conscious of the many benefits of this. It will take a bit of time, but the more you do it the more you'll see the rewards of managing your energy through a balanced approach to life. I want you to come away from this book realising that you have everything you need in yourself right now to make significant changes to your life.

We all have an enormous amount of potential, but we may find invisible barriers get in the way of fulfilling it: those niggles from our past that keep haunting us; the critical voice in our head that tells us we can't do it, that we aren't good enough, that we might fail or that people won't like us, and so on. It's frustrating and repetitive and it doesn't have to be that way. By getting caught up in these thoughts, you will find yourself struggling against a riptide, when you can find your flow in life simply by being aware of what's happening.

For me, achieving total energy awareness remains a work in progress, but it's been such a game changer in terms of how I feel. The things I don't want to happen still do occur, but my attitude to them has shifted. How I cope and handle situations has been completely transformed. In the past, life's stresses and intense feelings used to make me want to escape – and I'd find ways to do that. These days I am not afraid of my feelings, I breathe deeply and see them as pointers to help me understand myself and what's happening in my energy. I also now have the tools to sail through them unscathed and to return to a state of grace, where I feel like the world is on my side once more.

The important thing to remember in all of this is that you are in the driving seat and you have a tremendous amount of power. You have the capacity to create, direct and receive the energy you need to live the life that you want. There is so much you can do by yourself to make significant changes in your day-to-day life. Even if you only begin by committing to the morning energy routine (see pages 63–5) and make that your habit, you will gradually see an improvement in your life experience.

My wish for you, dear reader, is that guided by the insights and practices in this book, you will get to know yourself in a whole new way through your chakras. With this enhanced knowledge and self-understanding, you will learn to shed the burden of your heavy emotions easily and raise your vibration so that you too can find your flow. Once you are in the flow, the current will bring you more of life's good stuff, and all you have to do is enjoy it.

Get in Touch

Please visit www.thecalmery.com for more information about one-to-one healing sessions, reiki training, workshops or coaching with me, Sushma.

Consultations take place at The Calmery in Harley Street, London or anywhere in the world via Zoom and FaceTime.

hello@thecalmery.com

www.thecalmery.com

@thecalmery

Further Reading

Ann Marie Chiasson, *Energy Healing: The Essentials of Self-care* (Sounds True, 2013).

Richard Ellis, *Reiki And The Seven Chakras: Your essential guide* (Vermillion, 2002).

Anodea Judith, *Wheels of Life: The Classic Guide to the Chakra System* (Llewellyn Publications, 1987).

Hiroshi Motoyama, *Theories of the Chakras: Bridge to Higher Consciousness* (New Age Books, 2018).

Dev OM, *The Cosmic Energy & Chakras* (Om Foundation, 2015).

Alberto Villoldo, *Shaman, Healer, Sage* (Bantam Press, 2001).

Sanaya Roman *Spiritual Growth: Being Your Higher Self* (HJ Kramer, 1988).

Candace B. Pert, *Molecules of Emotion: Why You Feel the Way You Feel* (Simon & Schuster, 1999).

C. P. Fagundes, R. L. Brown, M. A. Chen, et al. Grief, depressive symptoms, and inflammation in the spousally bereaved. *Psychoneuroendocrinology*. 2019;100:190-197. doi:10.1016/j.psyneuen.2018.10.006

Valerie Ann Worwood, *Aromatherapy for the Soul: Healing the Spirit with Fragrance and Essential Oils* (The New World Library, 2006).

Tamara Driessen, *The Crystal Code: A Modern Guide to Crystal Healing* (Penguin Life, 2018).

Marie Kondo, *The Life-Changing Magic of Tidying*: *A simple, effective way to banish clutter forever* (Vermilion, 2014).

Acknowledgements

There are so many people to mention who have been a part of my journey, but I have to begin with my family, my foundations holding me up from within. To my father, for teaching me to question, be curious and live impeccably with absolute truth and integrity. To my mother, for showing me that softness and patience are strength. To my sister, for lighting me up and making me laugh anytime anywhere! The constant love, support and steadfast belief in me from you three are why I have been able to follow my calling. Your open-mindedness and willingness to join me in areas you don't understand has blown my heart away. Words are not enough – but thank you!

I have endless appreciation for all my spiritual teachers over the years: every single one has taught me something incredible, but I do want to mention a few in particular. Thank you to Sue Johnson, for seeing something in me at the very beginning and inviting me to learn reiki. Thank you also to Richard Ellis, my reiki teacher and mentor for well over a decade of guiding me and encouraging me, knowing before I did that healing would be more to me than just a hobby. Diana Cox, for introducing me to Holy Fire. Thank you to Alberto Villoldo, Marcela Lobos, Stephen Feely, Moritz Reimann, Dirk, Isabella and Maria Clara at the Four Winds School. Your incredible guidance and world-class teaching nurtured my shamanic calling. You showed me the aliveness in all things, a new way of existing in nature that completely transformed me. Thanks also to Master Dev OM, who led me home to my roots and opened my eyes to an alternative way of approaching energy, chakras and life in general.

A big squeeze to Ruby Warrington, for ongoing friendship and encouragement. From day one your influence has inspired me to be more 'me'. Cheryl Slater and Jill Urwin from She's Lost Control, who believed in me and gave me my first real opportunities to do healing. Eminé Rushton, for all your help in my path to being a writer. My agent, Valeria Huerta, thank you for showing up when you did and everything that you do to champion me. Huge thanks to the amazing team at Ebury for the opportunity, and to publishers Samantha Crisp and Laura Higginson and editors Muna Reyal and Sue Lascelles for being so easy to work with. Your kindness, patience and skill have made this whole experience very positive for me.

My darling friends, too many to mention – anyone who has cheered me on, read a draft or given me moral support, in particular Jules, Russell and Misha. To The Calmery students, clients and online community, you keep me going and give me my 'why', I'm so grateful for you all in my life.

A final shout-out to all the awful times that made me seek out ways to heal and evolve – thank you too. I needed all of you to write this book!

Index

Notes

SUSHMA SAGAR

Sushma is the founder of The Calmery, a Harley Street energy healing clinic, in London. She is a certified Reiki Master and Shamanic Medicine Healer with over 15 years' experience. She runs events and workshops in London. You can find her on Instagram @thecalmery.

MORE NOW AGE ESSENTIALS

BALANCE YOUR AGNI: ESSENTIAL AYURVEDA
By Claire Paphitis

BE WILD BE FREE: ESSENTIAL SPIRIT GUIDES AND GUARDIANS
By Catherine Björksten

BLOOM & THRIVE: ESSENTIAL HEALING HERBS & FLOWERS
By Brigit Anna McNeill

YOU ARE A RAINBOW: ESSENTIAL AURAS
By Emma Lucy Knowles

YOU ARE COSMIC CODE: ESSENTIAL NUMEROLOGY
By Kaitlyn Kaerhart